Nourishment
for
New Moms

© 2011 by Barbour Publishing, Inc.

Writing and compilation by Joan C. Webb in association with Snapdragon Group™, Tulsa, OK.

ISBN 978-1-60260-960-0

Published by Barbour Publishing, Inc., P.O. Box 719, Uhrichsville, Ohio 44683, www.barbourbooks.com

Our mission is to publish and distribute inspirational products offering exceptional value and biblical encouragement to the masses.

Member of the
Evangelical Christian
Publishers Association

Printed in the United States of America.

Nourishment
for
New Moms

Joan C. Webb

BARBOUR
PUBLISHING

Thank You

Thank you to the generous mothers who shared their new-mom stories of angst, joy, and reliance on God. To protect the women's privacy, I've only used first names and in some cases have changed names and details. Hopefully the readers will identify with these women's experiences and be inspired by the lessons they've learned.

Contents

A Word to You, Reader

New mom, I thought of you and prayed for you while writing these nine chapters. As you skim the table of contents, you'll notice that each chapter deals with a specific subject that new mothers face. Go directly to a section that interests you. You don't have to read the book in chronological order, but you certainly can. I know you're busy, so to make reading this book a little easier, I've divided each chapter into five sections.

1. ## What's Up, Mom?

   This first section introduces you to the challenging reality of each chapter's topic. You will find lighthearted stories to help you identify with the specific issue.

2. ## Who, Me?

   The second section guides you to answer the question: "How does this chapter's subject affect me and my family?" Life-coaching questions and exercises have been included to help you relate your story to the topic.

3. ## Been There—Done That

   In this section, you will read stories from members of the New Moms Club. These anecdotes include the experiences of women of all ages and backgrounds, as well as stories of mothers from scripture.

4. It's a Juggling Act

 The fourth section is filled with practical tips, tools, and ideas for balancing self-care with other-care. You are given opportunities to personalize these suggestions to your specific circumstances.

5. Safe in God's Arms

 Included in the final section are encouraging words from God and from other new moms who've trusted God with their confusing situations.

Read on for a little relief and nourishment in your role as mother to your sweet baby.

A mother's joy begins when a new life
is stirring inside. . .when a tiny heartbeat
is heard for the very first time, and a playful
kick reminds her that she is never alone.
ANONYMOUS

Chapter 1

You Are
Not Alone

What's Up, Mom?

Round-the-Clock Duty

"Mother, why didn't you tell me about this new-mom stuff? Warn me or something?" I chuckled as I swallowed my tears. I didn't want her—or anyone—to know how frazzled and inadequate I felt with this awesome, brand-new motherhood role I'd chosen.

As I looked into the eyes of my precious two-and-a-half-week-old baby girl, she screeched for who knows what reason. I mean I'd already fed her, changed her diaper, dressed her in a darling new outfit, loved on her, laid her down, picked her up, rocked her, swung her, hugged her, and taken her for a ride in the stroller.

Then I fed her again, changed another diaper, dressed her in a different but equally cute outfit (surely it would make her happy to know how good she looked!), kissed her, sh-sh-shushed her, put her in her crib, and waited what seemed like hours while I did a load of laundry. And when she didn't stop crying, I took her out of her bed to sit down in our favorite rocking chair (first making certain my pillow was strategically placed on the seat—I was still sore) where I sang to her, jostled her, and prayed. I hadn't had time to wash and style my hair since before labor started. Basically I had sacrificed my sanity on the altar of round-the-clock caring and nursing duty. What else did this bundle of preciousness want? I just felt so tired.

Mom's voice brought me back to the current noisy moment. "What good would it have done, honey?" This unexpected response from my normally quite understanding mom stopped me cold, and I didn't say anything else. Mom added something like: "She'll stop crying soon. You've done everything you can." Then we said our good-byes and finished the phone call. (I was grateful Mom had flown out to California to help during the first few days of Lynnette's life, but sad when she had to return to her own life, which included a full-time job, my dad, my two teenage sisters, and my brother who had moved back home.)

Reminiscing about that day when I asked Mom the "why" question, I now believe she was trying to say that she didn't "warn" me because she didn't want to burden me with the overwhelming reality about having a baby *and* that forewarnings wouldn't have stopped me from getting pregnant *and* that she didn't want to squelch my I'm-going-to-be-a-mom excitement. Just rereading that lengthy sentence (and the previous one describing my sanity-threatening attempts to quiet my infant) sends shivers down my spine. Those were long and exhausting new-mom days. In my mother's defense, I think she had been taught that any discussion about difficult or unpleasant matters made them worse, so in avoiding this kind of interaction, she was actually helping me. *Hmmmm.* Just between you and me, it really didn't help much.

Who Can't Boil Water?

What I really wanted was to not feel so alone. And I wondered if anyone had ever felt like I did, so exhausted and foggy-brained that I couldn't remember how to boil water. *Honestly!*

Besides feeling overwhelmed and underprepared, I was just a teeny bit anxious. (Who am I kidding? I was trying too hard to do it all just right and worried that I wouldn't or couldn't.) I wanted someone to talk to about my ideas, fears, joys, confusion, and questions, but my sisters were too young (and in Kansas), and we had only lived in Bakersfield for three months. I didn't have many friends my own age or know many babies since my husband held the new youth pastor position at a large church. (We were surrounded by teens!) And even though everyone welcomed us with open arms, I felt alone. Perhaps as a new mom—in your own unique circumstances—you feel alone sometimes, too.

Sobering Reality

Maybe you identify with a dedicated young mom named Patrice who said, "One of the most difficult aspects of new motherhood was the isolation I felt. I looked at other new moms and thought, *They have it all together. Why don't I?* Later I discovered that they were watching me and thinking the same thing. Who knew?"

It's not scientific, but according to my own survey, 90 percent of new moms feel overwhelmed, tired, and alone while adjusting to this new-mom lifestyle. I say 90 percent just in case there are women who never encounter any of the dilemmas I've just mentioned.

Please don't raise your eyebrow at me. A mom like that could exist out there—somewhere. Although I admit I've never met one.

At first the mystery and pure joy of motherhood overtakes you as you hold your cuddly newborn baby. Nothing has ever felt sweeter, more refreshing, or more exciting. (Well, that may be overstating it a bit if you've just experienced a grueling labor or delivery.) No matter what your initial experience, it doesn't take too many sleepless nights or dinnertimes served with wails (I'm referring to the baby's tears, yet I realize you might be crying into your soup, too) for most new moms to realize that this is a job you can't skip out on. No call-in to the boss for a sick day. You *are* the boss! There's no walking off this job whether you're exhausted or not. When the full reality of it all sets in, it can be pretty frightening.

God's Remarkable Plan

Although it may feel like you're alone, you aren't. God has provided help to get you through. *Really.* He loves you and cares that you're tired, scared, happy, relieved, overwhelmed, perplexed, or just want to ask a few questions of someone who has been there and done that. That's why He made human relationships—to "encourage each other and give each other strength" (1 Thessalonians 5:11 NCV).

Sometimes you're the one giving help and support, and at other times you're the recipient of those acts of nurture and love. You actually bring God joy when you accept nourishment from others. So go ahead and ask for what you need.

In addition, God is with you whether you have a human being nearby or not. God wants to nourish you with His love, peace, and comfort—even in the middle of the night when you long to pull the covers over your head instead of straining your tired back to lift a crying baby out of his crib.

When others aren't available to listen and reassure you, God is. He knows you're going down for the third time and gasping for air. He loves you the same on your confident days as He does in your anxious moments. Just as He promised His loved ones in Isaiah 41:10, He promises you: "Don't worry, because I am with you. Don't be afraid, because I am your God. I will make you strong and will help you; I will support you with my right hand that saves you" (NCV).

While you lovingly reassure and nourish your baby, God will powerfully uphold and guide you. It's God's remarkable plan for new mommies when they're feeling worn out and alone. Often He executes His plans in surprising ways.

Jane Is Surprised by God

Tired doesn't really describe it. I was exhausted trying to care for my two-week-old daughter, run after my lively two-year-old son, and manage the house. With my husband on a week-long business trip and my mom preoccupied with caring for my ailing father, I felt alone, overwhelmed, and, well, bone-tired. Danny left a red crayon in the pocket of his white shorts, which went through the washer and dryer, leaving red specks and stripes throughout the entire load of whites and caked crayon globs melted on the inside of the dryer.

"God, I just can't deal with this. I'm going to bed." I guess it wasn't a prayer drenched in faith; more like a desperate plea for help. After struggling through the night, that next morning I scanned the Sunday paper. In the fixit column was a tip about removing crayon from a load

of wash and the inside of a dryer. I'm not kidding! So I tried it and it worked like a charm. Can't remember the exact tip. But talk about concrete evidence that God was with me and supporting me.

How I needed His help that autumn! Brian traveled six out of eleven weeks and my dad died three months after Mari was born. Trying times, but God showed me in a remarkably tangible way that I was, indeed, not alone. I really don't remember much else about those first weeks of Mari's life (well, except maybe the morning Danny shared his stuffed animals with her by placing them in her bassinet and nearly cutting off her oxygen!).

Who, Me?

No Two Mommies Alike

No other baby is quite like your baby. No other mommy is precisely like you. You each have distinctive needs, wants, and personality quirks. Add in the fact that your family's circumstances are not exactly like any other family situation and you can end up feeling different (even odd) and isolated from others and their experiences.

Although all new moms share certain commonalities (responsibility for a little human being, fresh decisions to make, adjusting to the rigors of 24–7 infant care—to name a few) each woman has unique challenges. Toni said, "I felt utterly alone and different, and I *was* alone. We'd just moved into a new home in the country (miles from anyone or any store) and downsized to one car. I left a sixty-hour work week on the day I delivered my baby to sit at home totally alone with a very quiet baby who needed little extra care. I had no one to chat with, no work projects to accomplish, nothing really to clean in my brand-new house, no 'wheels,' and nowhere to go anyway. I got depressed, and the blues didn't leave for months."

Annette experienced an equally frustrating yet opposite dilemma. She gave birth to a demanding baby boy who ended up with colic. She rarely had a quiet moment, lived in an older home that necessitated frequent cleaning, endured constant comparisons between her infant son and the many other baby cousins, and received massive amounts of conflicting advice from friends and family. She almost crashed with the overload until her doctor encouraged her to do what was best for her and her son.

Debbie felt alone within her circle of friends when she gave birth to triplets. Loretta learned that her much-prayed-for baby daughter had Down's syndrome and felt alone in her shock. Janelle, a teenage single mother, wondered if anyone could understand the depth of her devastation. Adoptive mom Caryn received the call that a baby was available in just five weeks instead of the expected eleven months. Yikes! Talk about unprepared.

Then there was Linda who had a dreadful pregnancy and immediately upon delivering her baby son felt like a new woman. When she compared any postpartum challenges to her nine months of continual nausea, pain, and constant concern for the baby's health, postpartum won hands down.

Every woman experiences motherhood uniquely. So what about you? What's happening in your life right now? Hopefully the next few questions and exercises will help you assess your current situation. Armed with the insight that every new mom's circumstances are unique—and the assurance that God wants to guide you—you can gain the motivation you need to seek specific resources and make intentional decisions for finding the relief you, your baby, and your family need and desire.

Making It Personal

To help you assess your unique new-mom circumstances, circle or highlight (in the book or in your mind) the phrases that describe your particular situation.

I am a new mom. . .

- for the first time.
- with another child still in diapers.
- with an older child (elementary age, teens, or older).
- with more than one other child.
- whose husband travels with his work and is often gone.
- whose own family (mother, sisters, extended family) lives out of town or state.
- who has helpful/supportive family and/or friends nearby.
- who is single.
- who has been married under one year.
- who waited to have children until after the age of forty.
- who works outside the home part-time.
- who works outside the home full-time.
- with a chronic illness or disability.
- who is also in the midst of a major life change (death in family, move, job/career change, just got married, perimenopause).
- who is dealing with baby blues (or postpartum depression).

- with a ministry position or who has a husband in the ministry.
- who had a difficult pregnancy or delivery.
- of a baby with a disability or chronic illness.
- who is experiencing new-mom realities and challenges because I'm a foster mom who has agreed to nurture infants.
- Other: _____

_____

After skimming the above list and choosing the statements that depict your new-mom situation, you may have thought of other descriptors that help explain your unique realities and practicalities at this stage of your life. For example, Alicia was a new mom who was enrolled full-time in a master's program at a local seminary. Janice homeschooled her older children when she became a new mom for the fourth time. Bobbi's husband served in the military and was stationed in the Middle East when their first son was born.

When I was six months pregnant with our first, my husband and I moved 1,300 miles across the country where I didn't know anyone, had to find a new obstetrician and hospital, and then I thought I needed to pretend that none of this was a big deal! In addition to that misconception, I had another: I thought that since I was the firstborn of four, had helped in caring for my siblings, and had done a lot of babysitting during my teen years that it would all come easy for me. *Ha!*

- Think of three to five realities and practicalities about your specific current season and circumstances as a new mom and insert them on the blank lines of the I-am-a-new-mom list above.
- How do your unique realities and practicalities contribute to your sense of feeling overwhelmed or isolated?
- What are the blessings and joys in your specific circumstances? How do these encourage you and lessen your sense of aloneness?

It helps to consider the truth about your realities and practicalities so that you can make wise and intentional decisions about how to help yourself, your baby, and your family. If you have the inclination, time, or energy you might jot your thoughts in the margin of this book or in a journal/notebook you place near the rocking chair where you feed your baby.

Been There—Done That

Welcome to the New Moms Club! Whether you asked for an invitation or not, you're in! Most new moms feel exhausted, overwhelmed, and alone at times, yet each mother has her own story. Hearing other mothers' unique accounts—like Kimberly's below—can help you realize you are not alone, no matter what your circumstances.

Kimberly's Renewed Gratitude

The phone rang. I answered.

"Are you sitting down, Kimberly?" said my doctor. "I have some troubling news. There's something wrong with your son."

It was the day before my scheduled caesarean section to deliver our breech baby. My young mind swirled with an overwhelming sense of responsibility. It had been just a little over one year since I got married at the age of eighteen. Shocked by this news, I sat down.

"We don't know quite what the problem is, but the ultrasounds point to some sort of mental disability."

My mind, body, and soul flooded with fear. Immediately I determined to do whatever it took to care for this baby, no matter what his challenges might be. Yet I worried I wasn't ready for the demands of parenting a disabled child. With no time, energy, or knowledge to do anything else, I prayed—for myself, my husband, and my unborn son.

Timmy was born the next day. "Your son appears to be fine," my doctor announced. "Sometimes ultrasounds are misleading."

My husband and I breathed sighs of gratitude. Still the experience shattered my confidence.

I embarked on a journey—more like a mission—to prove to myself (and everyone else) that I could succeed at taking superior care of my precious little boy. I over-bundled and over-bathed Timmy. I never left the house without a perfectly organized diaper bag. My motto became Always Be Prepared. *Unfortunately, my efforts to be the perfect mom did not produce the prodigy I had labored so hard to create. My baby remained uncomfortable, unhappy, and uninterested in me.*

"I'm failing as a mom," I concluded. "It's just so hard." Timmy didn't really seem to enjoy being held. He just wanted to be in his swing or on his blanket under his little baby gym on the floor. When upset, he became inconsolable. He continued to struggle against any attempts I made to physically comfort him, screaming frantically for what seemed like no reason.

And then everything I ever feared came true. The specialists began telling me the same thing my doctor had said the day before Timmy was born: "There's something wrong with your son." My new-mommy role expanded, and I became an autism-mommy. All the holding, hugging, and hovering I did to guarantee that my son felt nurtured and loved actually irritated him. How could this be? *I felt anxious. Alone. I longed for any reassurance I could find. I needed hope.*

Gradually God helped me replace extreme fear with deepening faith. Often I read the words of Isaiah: "All your children shall be taught by the Lord, and great shall be the peace of your children" (Isaiah 54:13 NKJV).

Even now this message comforts me.

In the moments (and there are many) when my skills as a mother do not meet the challenges of raising a special-needs child, I call on God for wisdom and peace. He is exceedingly faithful to respond and reassure me as He did when He gave me that verse in Isaiah. And I breathe a renewed kind of gratitude.

So I'm Not the Only One?

Recently I asked a small group of women this question: "As a new mom, when did you feel most alone?" Here's what I heard:

- "My mother came to help me after I gave birth to my son. Then she left to go back to her own home, and my husband returned to his work on the same day. That was just a few months ago, and I still shudder when I remember how alone I felt that day," said Candace.
- "After my daughter was born, I felt eerily alone the day it dawned on me that this wasn't just a baby-sitting job. This was my new reality!"
- "I felt most alone whenever I was at home with just my new baby and me. I so missed the social and mental stimulation that I'd enjoyed with my job," shared Jeri.
- Becky's immediate response to my question was laughter— long and loud. "Oh, I don't know," she sputtered. "I'm sure I must have a few thoughts or stories after seven straight years of constant babyhood at my house. I mean I've had two

babies of my own and four foster infants. What does it mean when I can't give you a sensible answer? I'm just so tired, I can't even think!"

Even Jesus' Mom Didn't Have It Perfect

Millions of women throughout the centuries in various cultures around the globe have made it successfully through the birthing and nurturing process. Sometimes I think it's encouraging to know this truth, and then at other times I'm not sure how much it helps.

Every new mom has distinctive surprises, challenges, questions, and emotions. As you contemplate what causes you to feel like you're all on your own, reflect on the following story found in Luke 1:26–38. Notice how this woman coped with her unique brand of aloneness.

"Mary, you're a lovely young woman with a heart for God," said a surprise visitor named Gabriel. Visibly shaken by the words of this messenger, Mary (probably still a teenager) had no immediate response. "Don't worry," he continued. "God's chosen you for a unique mission. This news may seem strange, but you're going to be a mother. In fact, you're going to have a baby boy named Jesus, and He'll grow up to be great. God will make him a ruler—forever and for all people."

"It's not that I don't believe you. I do," said young Mary after she finally found her words. "I just wonder how this could be, since I've never been sexually intimate with anyone, not even my husband-to-be."

"Your baby boy is God's Son. God will make it happen. You can count on it."

Surely Mary's mind raced as she wondered what she would tell her fiancé, family, and friends. It's as though Gabriel realized how alone Mary felt, since he immediately told her that her postmenopausal cousin, Elizabeth, was going to become a miracle-mother, also.

Mary believed that God was with her, and she said so. Yet Mary also realized she needed human support. Exhibiting wisdom beyond her years, Mary made an intentional decision to reach out and share with new-mother-to-be Elizabeth. All the while she remembered the reassuring words of God's messenger: "The Lord is with you" (Luke 1:28 NIV).

Between a Rock and a Hard Place—with God

God cares about you, Mom, whether you are famous or unknown, rich or poor, happy or depressed, educated or a school dropout, single or married. He will seek you and find you whether you are alone or surrounded by loved ones, whether you feel ready or highly inadequate for this mothering role, and whether you are rested or exhausted. He will come to help you. He'll send someone or something to support you. Ask Him. Trust Him. He cares.

"Don't be afraid, I've redeemed you.
I've called your name. You're mine.
When you're in over your head, I'll be there with
you. When you're in rough waters, you will not
go down. When you're between a rock and a hard
place, it won't be a dead end—because I am God,
your personal God...your Savior. I paid a huge
price for you.... That's how much you mean
to me! That's how much I love you! ...
So don't be afraid: I'm with you."

ISAIAH 43:1–5 MSG

It's a Juggling Act

Balancing Self-Care with Other-Care

Wondering how to balance self-care with other-care? Well, that's understandable. You probably realize (all too well!) that it is your responsibility to take care of your new little one, and you want to do that. Also, you desire to still do all the things you used to do for your husband, family, and friends. That definitely leaves no time to take care of yourself. Still, in your lucid moments, you sense that you need to do something to rejuvenate yourself so you can continue to give out.

Practical Tips for Your Juggling Act

1. Join a mom's group.

Remember Patrice who thought she was the only new mom who didn't have it "all together"? When her son was about eleven months old, she joined a church-run playgroup and discovered that many moms feel alone and overwhelmed. "I wish I'd joined sooner," she said. "Mothers are a tight-knit group. We will listen to one another's stories of sleep-deprived nights and celebrate small milestones in our babies' lives. We share experiences that only another tired mother can understand." To find a mom's group in your area, check with your local church, library, YMCA, or the hospital where you gave birth.

2. Partner with your husband (if you have one).

When I came home from the hospital with my first baby, Richard said, "Wake me up if you need me. Let me know what you need."

And can you believe it, I didn't do it! Oh, how I wish I would have taken him up on his initial offer. I guess he soon assumed I could do it on my own and didn't need him.

Sometimes it may seem like the males in your life don't understand what you've been through or what you're feeling now. After all, their genes *are* different than your mommy genes. Still most husbands really do want to help. Share your needs with your guy and ask for his practical support.

If he walks away while you're still in midsentence, don't give up. Some of you might be tempted to yell or nag to get him to listen. Or if you're like me, you might withdraw and determine to do it all by yourself. Neither idea is a great one, yet you don't have to do this partnership perfectly. Ask God to help you be direct and loving, and then try again. Tell your husband that you appreciate him, and learn to accept his attempts to help and understand.

3. Stay in touch with friends.

Relationships do change when you become a mom. You don't have the time or energy you had in your pre-motherhood days. And you may not have as much in common with certain people as you did before. Still, some friendships truly can and will survive major life changes.

Use a little creativity to nurture these bonds. E-mail, Facebook, Skype, blogs, cell phones. . .all have their downsides, but they can be amazingly helpful for staying in touch. Even if you can only get together every few months, planning a friend-date can reduce your sense of isolation and give you something to look forward to.

4. Give Mom (or Sis) a chance to help.

Mothers and sisters who have children can be a good resource for gaining helpful parenting information. There may be times that you will disagree on how best to nurture your child. Yet since your mom (or sister) became a member of the New Moms Club before you, she may have some inside poop (pardon the pun) on changing diapers and other messy baby stuff. Candace said that what helps her stay grounded and not feel so isolated is to talk regularly with her mother on the phone.

5. Stay in touch with yourself.

Taking a break from outside activities for a while as you adjust to your new role is a healthy strategy. (Notice how often employers accept the value of maternity leave.) Many moms have expressed how reconnecting with their specific interests has helped save their sanity and curb that sense of isolation.

New mom Lynnette, a marathoner, schedules her busy days to include time for exercise and training. "When I'm out running by myself, I get reenergized," she shares. Mommy Anne honors her passion for music by taking time to practice and perform with the Phoenix Symphony Chorus. Leslie, a professional photographer, admits that juggling her photo shoots with taking care of a colicky new baby is tricky, yet she loves how the people-connection keeps her in touch with the creative Leslie that God has designed. Staying in touch with what makes you unique enriches you—and sets a wise example for your children.

6. Connect with God.

Motherhood is God's idea. Babies are God's idea. *You* are God's idea. He knows that mixing tired mommies and crying babies with family, work, and regular life equals everyday messiness and curtailed-time availability. As you're adjusting to your new God-given mommy role, He doesn't expect you to have the same kind of intense Bible studies and elongated quiet times you had previously.

God is gentle with you and wants you to be gentle with yourself. The prophet Isaiah wrote this of Jesus, the coming Messiah, "He will not crush the weakest reed or put out a flickering candle" (Isaiah 42:3 NLT). It's God's character to care when you feel weak and exhausted from burning the candle at both ends. He's a loving and patient Savior, not one who bullies you into better faith.

Consider trying one of these simple and practical ways to connect with the One who loves you more than you'll ever know:

- Place a devotional book next to the chair where you feed your baby. Read one short page at a time and let the words nurture you as you hold and nourish your infant.
- Read a few encouraging verses in Psalms while you rock your baby.
- Play praise music on your iPod or computer while you're bathing or dressing your little one.
- Share the Alphabet Game with your older children (or do it on your own!). In my book *The Relief of Imperfection*, I write these ideas: "Name what you're grateful for starting

with A and proceeding through Z. For example: Father, thank You for the Air we breathe, Birds outside my window, Clouds, and so on through the alphabet." My favorite adaptation of this idea is to praise God for His attributes and characteristics. For example: Lord God, I praise You because You are Awesome, Beautiful, Big (this doesn't have to be perfect!), Caring, Compassionate, Cool, Delightful, Defender, Excellent, Everlasting, Forgiving, Father, Freedom-Giver. (Just skip a letter if you can't think of something right away.) Alphabet Praises never cease to lift my soul!

- Practice shooting-prayers when you feel yourself gulping for air in the Sea-of-Engulfment. Sometimes "Help, Lord!" is the most genuine prayer you can pray.

- Consider purchasing a small notebook to leave by your nightstand or end table. Write any thoughts, feelings, and ideas down and form them into prayers. Grammar doesn't matter. Just connect with yourself and God.

- Take a nap and while you're drifting off to sleep, recite a verse such as, "I lie down and sleep; I wake again, because the LORD sustains me" (Psalm 3:5 NIV).

- Ask for what you need. It's your privilege and responsibility to make your needs known. Asking does seem to be harder for some women. Still the truth is: You don't have to do this new-mommy thing all alone. God provides ways for you to get support and help. (Remember when you ask, other people have the option to say yes or no, or renegotiate the way they provide.)

Although your life has become a juggling act trying to attend to the needs of a new baby as well as all your regular tasks and activities, there are intentional actions you can take. They will help you restore a semblance of balance to your days. God smiles as you practice your juggling!

Safe in God's Arms

I'm a walking zombie. I remember thinking and voicing these words after months of awakening with a crying, hungry baby up to seven times a night. I also recall feeling rather alone and wondering if anybody was listening. I never dreamed I'd be so tired. (Later we learned that Rich had chronic ear infections, resulting in temporary hearing loss for several years. No doubt this contributed to his restless sleep patterns.)

Even in my exhaustion, I knew God was with me. I believed my zombie days wouldn't last forever—and they didn't. God had His arms around me, even though I felt "too pooped to poop." (That's how I described myself!) So when I read Krista's e-mail about her new-mommy days, I identified.

Krista Says, "I'm Still Here!"

When my son was a baby, he went through a phase like most babies do, where he would become distraught if he couldn't see me. I'd walk into another room to grab something, and he'd cry. If I walked behind his bouncy seat where he couldn't see me for any length of time, he'd wail.

One day I was busy trying to finish some chores when it happened again. I walked out of view and he cried. When he couldn't find me, he screamed louder. I felt sad for him and wanted to reassure him. "Honey, it's okay," I said, "I'm still here. Just because you can't see me, it doesn't mean I left you."

I gasped. Oh, my, that's what God is saying to me. *Suddenly I felt the love and nurture of my heavenly Father. He assured me that even when I didn't see evidence of His presence, He was there. God never left. This was the first of many parenting* aha's *that God shared with me—and I'm incredibly grateful.*

Never Alone

The Lord answers, "Can a woman forget the baby she nurses? Can she feel no kindness for the child to which she gave birth? Even if she could forget her children, I will not forget you. See, I have written your name on my hand."

Isaiah 49:15–16 NCV

How precious to know for certain that God never forgets about you, Mom. He sees you when you're happy, rested, tired, confused, at peace, disappointed, overwhelmed—or renegotiating your roles and identity. He cares. You are *not* alone.

Now the thing about having a baby—
and I can't be the first person to have noticed this—
is that thereafter you have it.

JEAN KERR

Chapter 2

Where'd My Life Go?

What's Up, Mom?

Baby Changes Everything

"When this kid's mom comes to pick him up, my life finally can get back to normal." After weeks of interrupted nights and disoriented days, my friend Cathy craved the relief she'd feel when the mother of the baby she was caring for would come back and take over. Then it hit her: "I am this child's mom!" Cathy told me she remembers thinking how tired she was taking care of this little person who had invaded her home. She didn't know she had this subconscious thought until she realized the truth: Life would never be the same again.

Maybe you identify with Cathy's story or with Lynne who said: "I remember when I was sick with the flu. My husband was at work and all I wanted to do was crawl back into bed. But I had a fussy baby to feed. My stomach hurt, my body ached, my head pounded, and I just felt like yelling, 'I want my mommy!' I looked in the mirror, gulped back the tears, and announced to the haggard-looking young woman staring back at me, 'It's time to be the grown-up.' "

Am I Losing Me?

Your baby changes it all—forever. No more carefree days and spur-of-the-moment outings. No more leisurely mornings getting ready for work. (And you thought you were hurried before!) No more putting yourself first and foremost when you're sicker than a dog. (Okay, maybe you didn't do that!) Still, whatever your life was like *before baby*, things are quite different now.

When that tiny bundle arrived, you acquired a ground-shaking responsibility—the life of another human being. You're on active duty 24–7. It's an entirely new deal, and you're left wondering: *Where'd my old life go? Will I ever get it back?*

This new-mom career you've accepted offers excitement, challenge, and variety. You *know* motherhood is a noble, valuable profession, and you're proud to join the ranks. Yet in those rare quiet moments, you may miss the woman you were before and wonder if you're the only one who feels this way.

Maybe during those times you feel like Patrice (the talented young mom I mentioned in the last chapter) who says:

> *After all those years of being a successful student and worker at a job I loved, suddenly none of that mattered anymore. In my down moments I started to feel like a "nobody." Even though, intellectually, I knew that my new parenting gig was an important job and I* wanted *to raise my children, it was hard to have nothing to say to the inevitable questions of "What do you do now?"*
>
> *I had worked hard to obtain my graduate and master degrees—and I guess in some sense I felt like I had let down all those people who believed in me and encouraged me to make something of myself. Today I wouldn't trade being an at-home mother for anything. I love this new God-given career. It has allowed me to pursue other interests (such as writing), which I doubt I would have explored without this opportunity. Still I have my moments.*

Linda Shifts Focus

Or maybe you identify with Linda:

I wasn't sure I ever wanted children. After all, I knew it would change everything and tie me down. And then a simple, unexpected statement from a professor shifted my thinking. After I graduated from college and had started several businesses, I audited a post-graduate class on the topic of women's history. One day during our class discussion, I expressed my opinion about how having children would hinder me from realizing my potential, reaching my goals, and enjoying my God-given gifts.

Instead of agreeing with me, the professor (who had a long list of credentials behind her name) remarked, "On the other hand, perhaps having children will help you become the woman you were created to be, and you'd find fulfillment in that role."

I had never thought it of like that. I dropped my defenses and my heart changed. I began to feel what I hadn't allowed myself to feel: I really did want to have a child. *My husband and I talked about it all (he's always wanted kids) and after a while I got pregnant. Although I had a difficult pregnancy and adapting to my new role as mommy wasn't a snap, I learned that I actually love being a mom. I now have four children (the youngest is a one year old, so I'm a new mom all over again!). Indeed my life has changed. And surprise, surprise. This mommy role fits me.* Who knew? *Well of course, God did!*

Maybe you came to mommyhood reluctantly, or perhaps you planned for and dreamed of being a mother since you were a child yourself. Either way, you're likely to have experienced a similar reality: Life changes dramatically when you step into this new role. Some days are easier than others. And in it all you find reservoirs of strength and love within yourself that you never knew existed.

You don't forsake the real you with your past accomplishments, passions, and hopes because these will always be a crucial part of your personality and growth. Still the reality is that you added a new focus to your life when your baby arrived. Things are not the same and never will be.

A Brand-New Path

This reminds me of God's words to His children in Isaiah 43:18–19 (NIV): "Forget the former things; do not dwell on the past. See, I am doing a new thing! Now it springs up; do you not perceive it? I am making a way in the wilderness and streams in the wasteland."

Mom, God isn't advising you to forget who you are or what you've done. Instead He's encouraging you to concentrate on the exciting new role you've been given. You don't have to stay stuck in the past. You can move with joy into your future.

Even though the new is often overwhelming and can drain your energy, God is with you. He forges a road through uncharted territory and guides you when all you see ahead is thick brush. And when you feel parched, He offers you a cool drink of His reassuring guidance and love. Your life may have changed radically. But God hasn't bolted. He's right there, cutting out a path for you in this previously untraveled field where you're walking now.

Who, Me?

Not a Clue!

Okay, here's the deal. I admit I didn't know what pregnancy would be like. (I quickly found out! Richard called me the "Throw-up Queen.") Yet I did think I knew what to expect *after* the baby came. During my nauseating pregnancy days, I didn't worry too much about taking care of a new baby. After all, I reasoned that since I was the oldest of four kids, I knew more than the normal mommy-to-be.

My little sister is eleven years younger than I am. I babysat her and helped with chores; although thinking back now, I guess I primarily watched Mom do it. I'm quite observant, so I did learn how to change diapers, rock Karen, and give her a bottle—and I became good at deciphering what Mother might need in any given situation. When Karen got a little older, I helped with bathing and dressing her and fixing her hair.

Around age twelve, my cousin Jean and I formed a small business selling greeting cards and babysitting for our customers. (Born two months apart, Jean and I did everything together in our growing-up years, and our sister-moms often dressed us alike.) With all this practice through the years, I thought I knew a lot about babies when, at twenty-three years of age, I gave birth to our precious baby girl. *Not!*

Truth? I didn't have a clue what it felt like to be a mother—or what this life-change would mean. When the responsibility was all mine, my knees buckled under the burden. My mind went blank, and I nearly drowned under the weight of all that I had to know and do. Talk about being overwhelmed! *Yikes!*

Waaaaaay Different

In addition, my darling baby didn't always cooperate. She didn't sleep when I wanted her to (like at nighttime!). She pooped when it wasn't convenient to clean her up. She spit up at the most inopportune times: for example, on the way to church on her Dedication Day, I, the new youth pastor's wife, had to stand in front of the entire congregation in a smelly, stained dress. She cried (without fail) when I was supposed to be making dinner. I didn't know how to bathe her. (Yeah, yeah, I know that's what I thought I was so well-qualified to do, but this was waaaaaay different!)

I dressed her in a darling new outfit every time someone came to visit—and every time her daddy came home. (That was definitely one of my mommy-shoulds!) We had so much extra equipment to add to an already full one-bedroom apartment. It was a trick trying to figure out how to camouflage it all or put it away.

On top of all that, I didn't feel good. The episiotomy hurt. I was constipated, bloated. My mind was foggy. I had a reaction to the pain medication. Naps and meals seemed to be a tradeoff. If I took the time to fix myself something to eat while she was asleep, I missed my opportunity for a nap. If I napped when she was sleeping, I went hungry later. I had no time or energy for my part-time business or to help Richard with his youth pastor duties (I always had before).

When I went for three weeks without washing my hair, I almost lost it (my mind, not my hair!). It all left me wondering: *Where'd my life go—and where can I find it?* My life had changed all right; and although I adored my precious baby daughter Lynnette, I didn't know how to cope or ask for help.

I identify with author Beth Teitell in her book *From Here to Maternity*, when she wrote: "Because my mother and father and brother and I had so much fun together, I'd always associated parenthood with joy. Somehow I didn't realize the job had its share of drudgery, nor did I think about the fact that mastering the daughter role in no way meant I'd ace motherhood."[1]

I just *knew* that if I shared how I really felt, no one would understand. Everybody else looked (to me, at least) like they were coping quite well as new moms. But I was going downhill. I wish I would have connected more with other new mommies, but I thought I could do it alone. No, the more accurate reality is that I thought I *should* do it alone—and not bother anyone else.

Introvert/Extrovert Mommies

Part of this was because I didn't know how to communicate my needs to my husband or my friends (which were few since I was new to the community, remember?). And part of it was probably due to the fact that I'm a high introvert.

Every time I do a temperament assessment tool such as the Meyers-Briggs, I rank off the charts on the introvert scale. I *do* get reenergized by being alone—which, as a new mom, I was *not* since I

1 Beth Teitell, *From Here to Maternity* (New York: Broadway Books, 2005), p. 189–190.

now had a miniature human being attached to my hip!

I realize that highly extroverted women may approach new mommyhood's life-changing situations a little differently. For example, my friend Carol says she was "spoiled" as a new mom because her pastor–husband worked at home (and he helped when she needed him) and she had lots of church support. I realize that her circumstances may have adapted well to her new mommy needs. But I wonder if her outgoing ways made it more comfortable for her to reach out to interact with other moms and express her desires to her husband and family. Carol says:

The thing I remember helping the most was when the other mothers and I would share babysitting. We each took a morning or afternoon and rotated caring for one another's babies. Also, my husband and I discussed our needs and planned for him to take Mondays off (as a pastor that worked well), so he cared for the babies while I substitute-taught in the public school. It provided extra income for us, and I kept connected to the outside world and my gifts.

My family lived nearby and helped, as well. Because of all this encouragement and support, my entry into new momhood wasn't the huge shock it might have been for me and has been for others. I'm grateful.

Different Personalities—Different Approaches

What about you? Where do you register on the introvert-extrovert continuum? Knowing your personality preferences can help you maintain your uniqueness when life changes all around you. You can determine what you need, how to verbalize that need, and how to get the support that would fit your desires.

Outgoing Becky says, "When I feel overwhelmed and hurting, it helps me to 'shout out' to others. I don't suffer well alone or in silence. I make lots of noise until my friends arrive! I like empathy and a small group of friends to hold my hand in the dark with me. I yelp for help."

While introverted Mary writes, "I'm prone to want to retreat and be alone to renew my stamina when I'm feeling overwhelmed. I like to reflect on my options before I make a decision." Neither response is wrong, they're just different.

You are energized in one of two ways—through extroversion or introversion. Contrary to popular opinion, being an extrovert doesn't necessarily mean you are a boisterous party animal, craving to be out on the town every night, although you probably gain energy by being with other people or enjoying a group activity.

On the other hand, you may be refreshed by reflection, by being alone, or by enjoying one-on-one time with another adult. Exhibiting these natural tendencies toward introversion does not mean you wish to withdraw from society. Many women with inherent introverted preferences have highly developed social skills and make good teachers and communicators; it just takes more energy to do what doesn't come naturally.

My friend Dr. Jane Kise, an expert on personality types, says: "Extroverts get their energy from action and interaction while introverts get recharged through reflection and in-depth relationships.

This is huge for moms. If an extrovert starts thinking that being a mom is about devoting herself solely to her child and therefore she doesn't get out and about enough, she can get crabby. When an introvert doesn't find a way to have some time alone to reflect and recharge, she can get grumpy, too."

Making It Personal

On the next page, to help you determine your introvert/extrovert temperament, I'm including a simple exercise from a book I coauthored with Carol Travilla, entitled *The Intentional Woman*.[2] On the next page, circle the words or phrases that best describe what you prefer to do. Then place an X on the line between the words extrovert and introvert at the place where you believe you register on the continuum between the two extremes. For example, if you circled three words or phrases from each column, place your X in the middle. If you circled five words or phrases in the introvert column you would mark your X on the line closer to the word "introvert." Remember that we all can enjoy any of these activities at specific times, but usually not with equal confidence. Choose the phrases that indicate what you usually prefer, especially when you are under stress— whether it's positive or negative stress.

2 Carol Travilla and Joan C. Webb, *The Intentional Woman* (Colorado Springs, Colorado: NavPress Publishing Group, 2002), p. 67–68.

EXTROVERT —————— INTROVERT

EXTROVERT
I am recharged by:

- interaction
- activity
- working with a team
- conversation
- focusing on what is happening *around* me
- knowing what others are doing

INTROVERT
I am recharged by:

- being alone
- contemplation
- working alone or one-on-one
- writing
- focusing on what is happening *within* me
- knowing the idea/ motivation behind the action

Based on what you've learned about yourself in the above exercise:

- What specific support do you need right now as a new mom?
- What can you do to find that support?
- What small step will you take to help yourself?
- Who will you tell about your decision?

Family Changes

Whether you're an introvert or an extrovert, as your family grows you've probably noticed interaction of the various personality differences. Lynne felt the strain of her expanding family when she became a new mom again and brought her third child home from the hospital. She experienced difficulty trying to juggle everyone's emotional, mental, spiritual, and physical needs, but she couldn't put her finger on the problem or the solution.

She shared her confusion with a friend. "It feels like I brought twins or triplets into our house. With two kids I had one eye and one hand for each child *and* there was one parent for each child. But now, suddenly I'm outnumbered! *We're* outnumbered."

Lynne's discerning friend said, "Sounds like you feel that just because you've done this mothering career for several years that you should know how to make it all work this time. But the reality is that you're in a completely new situation. You've not only brought a new baby into your home, but you now have four new relationships. You're all trying to adjust to the new addition, and it's not easy."

Then she explained that when there are three people in a family, there are three relationships. Add another person and there are instantly six relationships. With the addition of another human being, ten relationships show up each morning. When there are six people in a household, there are fifteen relationships to track. It actually gave Lynne relief to realize that she now reigned as the matriarch of a domestic castle where ten relationships needed nurturing. She relaxed and gave herself a break.

What About Your Family?

Take a moment to look over the following Relationship Chart. Circle the scenario that best matches your situation.

RELATIONSHIP CHART

3 People (1 baby)	=3 Relationships	1. Mom with Dad 2. Mom with Baby 3. Dad with Baby
4 People (1 new baby makes 2 children.)	=6 Relationships	1. Mom with Dad 2. Mom with Baby 1 3. Dad with Baby 1 4. Mom with Baby 2 5. Dad with Baby 2 6. Baby 1 with Baby 2
5 People (1 new baby and 2 other children makes 3 dependent ones.)	=10 Relationships	1. Mom with Dad 2. Mom with Baby 1 3. Dad with Baby 1 4. Mom with Baby 2 5. Dad with Baby 2 6. Baby 1 with Baby 2 7. Mom with Baby 3 8. Dad with Baby 3 9. Baby 2 with Baby 3 10. Baby 1 with Baby 3
6 People (1 new baby and 3 older children make 4 babies of differing ages to mother and love.)	=15 Relationships	1. Mom with Dad 2. Mom with Baby 1 3. Dad with Baby 1 4. Mom with Baby 2 5. Dad with Baby 2 6. Baby 1 with Baby 2 7. Mom with Baby 3 8. Dad with Baby 3 9. Baby 2 with Baby 3 10. Baby 1 with Baby 3 11. Mom with Baby 4 12. Dad with Baby 4 13. Baby 3 with Baby 4 14. Baby 1 with Baby 4 15. Baby 2 with Baby 4

In what way does this information help you understand how your life has changed? How can you be gentler with yourself today?

Been There—Done That

New moms are often astounded at how their lives change after having a baby. It surprised Anne when she gave birth to her first son, and Julie found that becoming a mother was no fairy tale.

God Sends Anne a Gift

"How is it going?" asked the hospital nurse who called to follow up on my recent labor and delivery at the hospital just blocks from my home. I doubt she suspected what would happen next.

"Waaa-waaa-waaa," I exploded into the phone. *"It's horrible! I—I—I d–d–don't know what to do. H–h–he cries all the time. I'm so–o–o–o tired I can't move."*

"You've got to get that baby on a schedule," she scolded into the receiver. Her words were not *helpful to me. They merely added more ammunition to the ever-increasing arsenal of advice I'd already received from friends, family, neighbors, and acquaintances. Everybody had a different opinion. Nothing worked. I didn't have a clue what to do. I used to be a competent music teacher leading twenty-five to thirty children each day. Now all I could do was cry.*

Then it happened. God sent me a gift. I talked with an understanding Lamaze mommy and she said simply, "Anne, aren't you ever hungry between meals?"

"Uhhhhh. Yes. S–s–s–sure," I blubbered.

"Well, your baby is, too. So just relax and feed him. When he wants

*to eat and you can, nurse him." Somewhere in my foggy brain those
words rang true for me. So I began to breastfeed him when he appeared
hungry instead of trying to squeeze him into a schedule that worked for
other mothers. Things got better. I settled down. My baby settled down.
To this day, I thank God every time I think of that patient and wonderful
woman who told me I could follow my mommy intuition and do what I
felt best for my own child.*

Julie Gets Thrown into the Deep End

*I was thrown into the deep end of motherhood. Just three weeks after our
wedding, my husband and I brought home our adopted eight-month-old
baby. My great-niece needed a home, so a week after our wedding, we
offered to adopt her, fully expecting that the process would take months to
finalize. It didn't. I went from single career girl to married stay-at-home
mom in less than a month's time.*

*Instead of running my own business, I suddenly spent hours—and
hours—every day, rocking my new baby. We both struggled to adjust;
she to new parents and a completely new environment, and I to a totally
different life. So I just held her while my world tumbled around me.
I tried to figure out how to cook dinner every night, keep the house
somewhat clean, raise a child, and sort out my brand-new identity as
wife—and mother—all at once.*

*I felt like I was just getting into the swing of things when I got
pregnant with our second child. Sadly, I had a difficult pregnancy
including three months of bed rest. During that time all I could do was
cuddle my daughter since I couldn't get out of bed.*

When our son was born, our daughter had a really hard time adjusting to a new baby brother in the house. She exhibited bursts of jealousy. I couldn't turn my head away because she acted out by trying to hurt the baby or making a mess. I spent about six months sitting with the two of them on my lap, just holding them.

Since then I've had to return to full-time work outside the home. In the evenings and on weekends, my toddlers and I still love to snuggle. Life is definitely different than it was a few years ago. I treasure each moment I spend with them, because I realize my son and daughter will soon be in school, on their way to becoming teenagers and hopefully happy, productive adults.

Life Changed, but Not in the Way I Thought It Would

It's not just contemporary women who encounter major surprises as they contemplate becoming a mother—or not. In ancient Bible times, Hannah dreamed of having a baby. Although she and her husband loved one another deeply, she longed to strengthen their bond with a child. When she failed to conceive year after year, she couldn't hold back the tears—even in public places.

Hannah begged God to answer the longing of her heart. She even promised that if she did get pregnant and have a son, she would give him back to God's service for the rest of his life. Hannah's dream came true. She delivered a son and they named him Samuel. Giving birth to Samuel changed her life. She gained respect in the eyes of her family, friends, and culture.

Then because Hannah was a woman of integrity, she kept her

promise to God and, after nursing Samuel for several years, took her beloved young child to God's house to grow and serve. Her life changed again. No doubt with a heavy heart she left her son that day. Surely in her younger days, she never dreamed that becoming a mother would include such challenging and heart-wrenching decisions. Yet one thing never changed for Hannah. In the good *and* the bad times, Hannah prayed.

Becoming a new mom can be a difficult process with all the twists and turns that result in life changes that you never planned. Your journey may involve grieving your former self or the loss of your plans as you envisioned them. Some days you may want to celebrate and other days you may need to cry. Although it won't always be easy, you can learn to communicate with God in the midst of your planned and unplanned life-changes, just as Hannah did. (See 1 Samuel 1:2–28.)

I'm bursting with GOD-news!
I'm walking on air.... Nothing and no one
is holy like GOD.... GOD knows what's going
on.... He rekindles burned-out lives with
fresh hope, restoring dignity and respect
to their lives....The very structures of
earth are GOD's.... He'll give strength.
1 SAMUEL 2:1–3, 8, 10 MSG

It's a Juggling Act

What's a Woman to Do?

It happens to most (and maybe all) mothers. There comes a day sometime after the birth of your first child when you stumble out of bed in the morning (or in the middle of the night) and you don't even recognize your own feet, much less your face. You haven't had a full night's sleep in weeks (maybe months), and you're exhausted. Your relationships with your partner, mother, sister, extended family, friends, colleagues, and employer have all changed. Your own priorities are shifting.

The 24–7 needs of your baby have taken center stage and almost everything else has been relegated to the wings. If you're like most other moms, you may stare in the mirror and ask, "Who exactly am I now that I'm a mother?" Your life has changed. Some adjustments you cherish. Others send you reeling. What's a woman to do?

Here are a few practical suggestions. Which one might be helpful to you?

Be Patient with Yourself

When you accept a challenging new career position in an area where you've had scant experience, you don't expect to be a complete success your first day on the job. Give yourself the same consideration for your new motherhood position. For many women it will take six months to a year (sometimes longer) to be comfortable in your new role. Avoid berating yourself when some aspects of mothering don't come automatically. In time, you'll reach your stride and your intuition will take over. You'll learn what your baby's different cries mean, and how to soothe him (at least most of the time). Give yourself time to adjust.

Nurture a Personal Interest

"Cultivating a hobby or personal creative passion may seem counterintuitive because you have probably never been busier in your life than you are right now. Yet in your search for identity, it is important to have something you can call your own," shares Patrice. I agree that dedicating at least some time to something that interests you and will engage your mind is a worthwhile idea.

Do you like to read? Keep a magazine or book handy. It is amazing how much reading you can get done one paragraph at a time! Do you like to take photos? This is a wonderful time to put those skills to work taking pictures of your baby. If you enjoy writing, keep a casual journal. Remember, no one's grading it.

Whatever you enjoy, there's probably some way to integrate it into your new life. Tia continued to honor her love for music by teaching a few piano students while Daddy watched the baby. After Lori recovered from delivering her baby, she gradually resumed her jogging routine on mornings when her husband could go into work a little later. Sarah began gardening again as soon as she felt up to it.

If renewing a previous interest is not feasible, then consider slowly integrating something new into your life. Learning a fresh skill or continuing an old one can energize you and help you realize that while you are a mom, you are also a talented and creative woman.

Find a Life Coach or Coaching Group

To help you move past negative thinking and find fulfillment, purpose, and balance in your life as a new mommy, consider engaging the services of a mommy coach or life coach. (Check online or ask your friends at your church, club, or work for references.) If hiring a life coach is not possible for you, try coaching yourself. Here are two powerful coaching questions to ask yourself when you feel overwhelmed by trying to juggle it all:

- "Since I'm going to take care of my baby anyway, how can I make it more fun today?" Then ask this again the next day until you acquire the habit of developing more lighthearted options.
- "What do I need right now? What do I want?" If you find yourself answering repeatedly with an "I don't know" response, ask this one additional question: "Okay,_____ (fill in your name), if I *did* know, what would I need or want?" You may find your response enlightening!

Don't Read This Book in Chronological Order

Instead of plowing through this book, open up to the table of contents and choose the topic that attracts your attention at the moment. Read that chapter next. After responding to the "If I did know, what would I need or want?" question, locate the topic that best fits your felt-need and read about how other new moms have coped. There's no perfect way to learn. And you don't have to do it all in the next few days or weeks. Take your time.

Safe in God's Arms

Not every little girl longs to be a mother. (Remember Linda's story at the beginning of this chapter?) However, I often do hear women—whether they've had longtime careers outside the home or not—share their growing-up-to-be-a-mommy dreams, which are all amazingly similar to Donna's story.

From as far back as I can remember, I dreamed of being a mother. I could hardly wait for that day to arrive. I loved being pregnant. I wasn't overly concerned about the pain of labor and delivery, viewing it merely as a means to the end: me fulfilling the lifelong dream of mommyhood. So you can imagine my shock when I felt overwhelmed with fear and insecurity after my baby girl was born. Putting it bluntly: I was scared to death. Now at last a mother, I was supposed to know exactly what to do and how to meet my baby's needs. I didn't. I never fathomed how my life could change so much.

Every day as a new mommy you face decisions, situations, emotions, relationship dilemmas, and exhaustion levels unlike any you've experienced previously. That's how it was for me, too. I longed for reassurance that I could do this, that I'd make it through. Then I read a Bible verse that calmed my heart and gave me hope.

*"I will lead the blind by ways they have not known, along
unfamiliar paths I will guide them;
I will turn the darkness into light before them
and make the rough places smooth. These are
the things I will do; I will not forsake them."*

ISAIAH 42:16 NIV

I couldn't see ahead and didn't know the best solution to these
new challenges. It was just all so unfamiliar to me—and my husband.
I knew I needed a wise, competent, and caring guide. One who knew
the road ahead. One who could take my hand and lead me down a
dim and bumpy path.

So I took God up on His promise to guide me. You can, too.
He knows your fears and your humanness. He loves you anyway. He
wants to be your walking companion during these unfamiliar—and
often messy—new-mom days. You're safe with God. You can ask Him
that haunting question, "Where'd my life go?" Tell Him what you're
feeling. Pause to listen to His answers. He's not going anywhere.

Relax, everything's going to be all right;
rest, everything's coming together;
open your hearts, love is on the way!
JUDE 1:2 MSG

Chapter 3

Decisions, Decisions

What's Up, Mom?

Pros, Cons, and Ramifications

"Here's your baby, ma'am." The nurse on duty handed me my few-hour-old baby girl, Lynnette. "It's time for her feeding."

I gazed into those precious blue eyes. To me she was beautiful, even though her head was still misshapen and forceps marks marred her cheeks. However, I must have had a blank look on my face, because the nurse said, "Well, do you want to try breastfeeding your baby?"

Uhhh, I guess so. Thoughts whirled in my head, but I asked no questions. Still foggy-brained from the twenty-four-hour labor, medication, and forceps delivery, I nodded yes.

The nurse positioned Lynnette against my chest, and the baby latched on. It worked. *Amazing.* Then I nursed her again—and just kept right on going. (I know it's not quite so simple for some new moms. More about that later.)

Although I had read the pregnancy books and had gone to some classes, I don't remember being encouraged to breastfeed my baby or *deciding* ahead of time to do so. As the first of four children, I didn't have an older sibling role model; and although Mother may have assumed I'd try nursing, we didn't discuss it.

It was one of many choices I faced as a brand-new mom, and it just seemed right for me at the time. And it was. I loved it. (I know nursing is not the best decision for every new mom. Considerations such as adoption, health problems of the baby or mom, medication restrictions, baby unable to nurse, and logistical issues pertaining to work and scheduling all factor in to help a woman make her decisions about formula or breastfeeding.)

Yet for me it meant no feeding paraphernalia to take on road trips, not needing to buy formula, and readily available nourishment for baby always at the correct temperature. It also meant that Lynnette got used to *me* and wouldn't take a bottle easily. Actually, she never did get used to that bottle, and I had to try to schedule appointments whenever she wouldn't be hungry.

It got Daddy off the hook in the feeding department for months! I had the leaking boobs issue to deal with also, but I soon learned that was merely part of the nursing game. This leads me to the new mom's inevitable and ever-present reality: *Each decision she makes has pros, cons,* and *ramifications.*

A Gazillion Decisions

How to nourish your new baby is merely one of the gazillion (or so it seems!) decisions bombarding you as a new mom. Who would have imagined there would be so many choices to make?

- Home birth or hospital?
- Go back to work or take a leave of absence?
- What to name our new little family member? (And whether to keep our ideas a secret or let family and friends in on the process?)
- How long should I stay in the hospital?

- Daycare, mom care, or stay-at-home-daddy care?
    - Whether to work part-time away from or at home?
    - Which pediatrician to trust my baby's well-being with?
    - Do we circumcise our baby boy or not?
    - How to prepare my firstborn for a new little home-invader?
    - Put my baby on a schedule right away? Let him determine when he's hungry?
    - If I breastfeed, what foods or medications should I avoid?
    - What tests for my baby should I allow in the hospital nursery?

And that's just for starters. The decisions seem endless. So you thought choosing which college to attend or what house to buy were big decisions! Admittedly those *were* important choices that you made. Still the considerations, choices, and decisions involved with new mommyhood seem to shadow any former ones (at least while you're in the midst of making them). Unfortunately many of these baby decisions must be finalized when you're sleep deprived, sore, blurry brained, and emotionally haywire.

In case you're wondering what other specific questions crowd into a new mom's mind and fight for attention, here are a few more:

- What crib to buy?
- Which diapers to use?
- Which nursing bra works best for me?
- What supplies do I really need?
- Is he getting enough nutrients?

- What thermometer to use?
  - Should I keep her near us in our room at first or in a crib in her own room?
  - How soon should I take him out in public?
  - How do I find a good babysitter?
  - Should I trust a babysitter?
  - Does he really need a dozen onesies?
  - Should I take a chance on him catching germs from other kids in the church nursery?
  - Am I a bad mommy if my baby gets a diaper rash? What should I do if he does?
  - Start solids at four months old, six months old, or later?
  - How can I keep her from spitting up all the time?
  - When should I cut his fingernails?
  - Should he sleep on his back or on his tummy? (Medical experts have developed definite ideas about this one within the last few years.)
  - Pacifier or not?
  - What car seat do I buy? (You and your family will want to check out your state's specific requirements.)
  - What inoculations should I permit my baby to have?
  - Naps on a schedule or just whenever?
  - And the BIGGIE: What if I make the wrong choice and my baby has to have years of counseling later to undo the harm?

Oh, the Pressure!

How do you make all these decisions? It is a lot of pressure, and it's not always easy to know what to do. What works for one mommy might not work for another. What works for you one week may not work as well in a month.

Obviously some of the decisions are heavier than others. The name you choose for your baby will be with him for life. Of course, he could always change it later in a court of law. (Before you burst into tears at the mere idea of that possibility, remember the statistics are on your side, Mommy. Most likely he won't do that, so you can stop sniffling now!)

Other decisions just won't matter that much a few years from now. Really. For example, one mommy took weeks trying to decide whether she'd use cloth or disposable diapers. She chose cloth ones. With her first child, she made sure she changed the diaper every hour, whether he needed it or not. When her second child was born, she decided disposables would work just fine.

In addition, she altered her strict diapering schedule a little, changing her infant daughter's diaper every two to three hours, *if needed*. And when the third child arrived, she decided to change him right before others started to complain about the smell or when she saw the disposables sagging around his knees. All three children grew up fine, becoming typical teenagers and responsible young adults.

No Flawless Choices

I don't wish to step on your toes, but you won't always make perfect decisions 24–7—either as a new mom or in the years to come. It's just too much to expect from a mother's finite brain. (Or a dad's, for that matter!) Now if you were God, then you'd make flawless choices all the time in every situation and the results would be just what you dreamed for everyone and everything. But alas, that's not reality. You can only do the best you can with the information, circumstances, time, and energy available to you at the moment. The good news is you have the awesome privilege of giving what you can't control or figure out to the only truly perfect One, God Himself.

Trust GOD *from the bottom of your heart;
don't try to figure out everything on your own.
Listen for* GOD*'s voice in everything you do,
everywhere you go; he's the one who will
keep you on track. Don't assume that
you know it all. Run to* GOD*!*

PROVERBS 3:5–7 MSG

Who, Me?

Baby Counts, Too

Perhaps you believe that *everything* (your child's health, character, spiritual life, education, choice of mate, and personality development) depends on *your* decisions. The truth is, although your choices and behavior are important to the welfare of your child, the baby herself (or himself) has a say in those outcomes as well.

Recently I talked with a mother who told me a personal story to illustrate this. Bonnie has twins: darling little blond-headed girls. She determined to raise them both exactly the same way she raised her older son. She made similar decisions about many things and since she was a pacifier advocate, Bonnie offered both her baby daughters a "binky" at the first sign of a distressed whimper.

Darla loves her pacifier and can easily comfort herself as long as she can put her chubby hands on her little nipple-shaped constant companion. But Denise never accepted it. She made faces at the little rubber thing from the first moment I touched it to her lips. I had a plan, but Denise's personal preferences didn't go along.

Oh, and by the way, Darla seems to appreciate a regularly scheduled naptime in her crib, while Denise would rather play it by ear and just fall asleep in the stroller. And regardless of what I eat, Denise spits up nearly every time I nurse her and Darla hardly ever is the reason I have to change my shirt several times a day! Thus, my theory at this point: Some decisions are just not earth shattering and definitely not worth losing sleep over or arguing with your mom about.

A Biggie or a Smallie

A few decisions do bear more weight and often render results that could become turning points in your life and the life of your child. (A *turning point* is something that happens that *turns* your life in one direction or another, for better or worse, toward or away from something where the future is not going to be a continuation of the past. It may include the choices of another person and/or events and circumstances that are out of your control, as well as major decisions you make such as what career path you'll follow, what state or country you'll live in, or who you'll marry.)

So what's happening with you right now? Are you facing a life-altering (turning point) decision such as "Shall we have another child? Now? Later? Never?" Or is your current dilemma something like: "Who is going to cut baby's fingernails today so he won't scratch his face in the middle of the night again?" (And because the last time you tried the nail-cutting feat, he waved his arms and screeched uncontrollably, it's understandable that you're not looking forward to repeating this scenario!)

Making It Personal

To give you an idea of the decisions you're currently facing at this moment, reflect on the questions below. (Take it easy! You don't have to answer each question. Just use these as helpful guides for gaining clarity about where you are right now, what decisions are pressing, which choices are fairly simple, and what you can put on the back burner for a while.)

- What bothers or concerns me right now? (Hint: Think about what is preoccupying your thoughts at the moment.)
- What won't matter much next week? Or next month?
- What do I really want to do about _____ _____? (Fill in the blank with your response to question number 1.)
- What are my options regarding _____ _____? (Fill in the blank with your response to number 3.)
- Who can I ask to share this decision-making load with me?

Take a deep breath. Inhale for five seconds; pause, and then exhale for five seconds. Now again. Breathing deeply makes decision making just a little lighter. Yes, I know that breathing slowly and consistently is difficult when you're feeling pressured, exhausted, and confused by the steep learning curve you've encountered with this new-mommy position. So since shallow breathing tends to come more naturally during these times, you may want to be deliberate about slowing down your internal motor by taking some deep breaths.

Who's in Charge Here?

People—friends, mentors, parents, aunts, sisters, authors, experts— have many ideas and suggestions for you. It can get overwhelming. How can you make decisions that work for you and still be grateful for others' helpful input?

That's what Lori wondered. With her first baby, she tried to follow the rules verbatim. Yet sometimes she felt that the rules fit the medical community more than they fit her.

Lori Shifts Her Focus

I had my baby girl in the hospital where I was induced into labor, talked into having an epidural, and almost a C-section. When it came time for Baby Vivian's first "wellness" visit, my back was out and I hadn't slept in three nights. I didn't want to go, but I thought I had to, so I did. It was painful. It never occurred to me to reschedule the appointment.

Once I got back home, I did what I was told, including putting my baby on her back, even when she obviously enjoyed being on her tummy. Trying hard to comply with all the rules and do it just right, I jumped every time she stirred. I had three bottles ready in the fridge to be heated at a moment's notice when it dawned on me that heating a cold bottle took longer than making one from scratch.

One day while icing my own aching back and crying from exhaustion, I wondered why I was driving myself crazy trying to adhere to everyone else's ideas. When my sister called to ask if she could stay over and take a night shift so I could rest, I said, "Come!" That one act of kindness probably saved me! I needed help; yet what I didn't need was to focus merely on doing what others thought I needed but clearly did not work well for me.

So when I became a new mom the second time, I made my own intentional choices. I had my baby on a real bed at a birthing center and although it was the hardest thing I've ever done, I didn't have the added stress of being induced, enduring an unwanted epidural, or staying too long in a sterile environment. Then I made my own appointment on my own schedule for that "wellness" visit and planned upfront to accept my sister's help for an entire week. I focused on what was most comfortable for me and my baby. It was all quite freeing to make the decisions that I had control over while at the same time accepting help from others. I could relax and enjoy my family more.

Been There—Done That

Every woman has unique needs and desires associated with her new-mom role. Pain levels vary for each mother. Babies have distinctive needs. In addition, the circumstances in your family are different than those in your best friend's or doctor's family. Although others' experiences and ideas can be helpful, there's no law—written or unwritten—that mandates how you must approach your new career as the mommy of your baby.

One young mom said, "I decided I'm not going to get a gold medal for doing this completely as a natural birth, so I asked for an epidural." Another mother found joy and fulfillment in experiencing every moment of her baby's birth process and having the opportunity to control her body, breathing, and pain on her own. Consequently she hired a midwife and gave explicit handwritten instructions to all medical personnel about what she did and did not want during her baby's birth process. Although you may not wish to do this, it does illustrate the fact that you *do* have options.

Bath-Time Decisions and Other Dilemmas

Remember my "blank stare" hospital story about my breast-feeding decision? Well, that wasn't the only decision I faced in the hospital. It's been quite a few years now, but I vividly recall feeling overwhelmed about how I was going to bathe my new baby girl. (Even though I thought I knew about such things because I had helped with my baby sister, I found that it wasn't the same when it was all up to me!)

I can recall the panicky questions jumping in my brain when I contemplated going home and being faced with having to give her a bath. How would I do it? *Where* would I do it? In the kitchen sink, bathroom sink, tub? Should I buy a plastic baby bathtub? What soap do I use? How often does she need a bath? What if she gets too cold?

Then the nurses invited me to a "Bathing Baby" class. And I couldn't decide whether to go. I was in pain, still had a catheter, and didn't feel like walking down the hall. *What if I was the only mom who didn't know how to give her own baby a bath? What if I'm the only one who shows up? Will I look dumb?*

Being overly nervous and indecisive was not my normal mode. So what was up with my decision freeze? Since that day in the hospital, I've talked with numerous intelligent and capable women who admit to having similar concerns about the bath time, diapering, scheduling, washing baby clothes, and when-to-sleep decisions. It just seems to go with the tired new mom's unfamiliar territory. So if you ever over-ruminate about any of these types of decisions, give yourself a break! You're in good company.

Who's Working Where?

Maybe you're facing a major decision such as "Should I go back to work or stay home with my baby?" Or "*When* should I go back to work?" Or "Will Daddy stay home with our son while I go back to my position?" Or "Who will take care of the baby while I'm at work?" Please know that you are one of many women facing a similar dilemma. For some of you it may be a relatively easy decision. Perhaps a given. For others it might be one of the hardest decisions you've ever tackled.

When I asked mothers for their thoughts on this issue, one wise mom wrote, "Whether you are a working mom, a stay-at-home mom, or something in-between, the important thing is for you to make the best decision for you and your particular set of circumstances. The difficult part is that your initial decision often has to be made before your baby arrives. It's hard to know how you will feel about turning your baby over to another caretaker or about leaving paid employment until after the baby arrives. The good thing is that nothing is set in stone."

Read information about the pros and cons of each option, discuss it with your husband, journal your thoughts, and pray for guidance. Then determine your choice about working outside the home, avoid second-guessing your decision, give it your full commitment while adjusting, and then allow yourself to change your decision later if you and your family discover it just does not work.

In the popular book *What to Expect the First Year*, authors Murkoff, Eisenberg, and Hathaway write, "Whatever choice you make, it's likely to require some measure of sacrifice. As committed as you might be to staying home, you may, nevertheless, feel a pang or two (or more) of regret when you talk to friends who are still pursuing their careers. Or as committed as you might be to returning to your job, you may experience regret when you pass mothers and their babies on their way to the park while you're on your way to the office."[3]

Moses and His Mom

Jochebed, a young mother in Bible days, faced a major decision after her son Moses was born (see Exodus 2:1–10). Yes, he's the same Moses of "Let My People Go" fame! Because of the Egyptian king's recent edict to kill all Israelite boys, Jochebed knew her son was in danger. She could have panicked and locked herself into black-and-white thinking, such as: *He'll die if I don't succeed in continuing to hide him perfectly for the next few years. It's one or the other. I have no choice.*

Instead, this creative new mother steadied herself, undoubtedly asking God for guidance. Then she turned her back on the either/or mindset and explored her options. After crafting a little boat-basket for baby Moses, she handed him to his big sister with explicit instructions to put him in the river near where the Egyptian princess bathed.

Miriam kept an eye on her baby brother from behind a nearby bush, and when she saw the princess smile at the baby and talk to her maids about him, she stepped up. "Would you like me to find a proper nanny who can nurse this baby for you?"

"Good idea. Go."

What happened next is amazing. Miriam brought Jochebed to the Egyptian princess who hired Moses' own mother to nurse and care for him. At the same time, Jochebed had the privilege of nurturing, loving, and instructing her son in the ways of God during

---

3 Heidi Murkoff, Arlene Eisenberg, and Sandee Hathaway. B.S.N., *What to Expect the First Year* (New York: Workman Publishing. 2003), p. 713–714.

his formative years. Much later, after being educated in the Pharaoh's extravagant schools and culture and living as the princess's adopted son, Moses remembered what His birth-mother had taught him. He aligned himself with the Hebrew people and became God's choice to deliver His people from slavery.

A previously unknown yet courageous new mother overcame her fear of making the wrong decision, to think outside the box and find options. She stepped up in faith to partner with God to change history. Although your situation may not be quite as dramatic as Jochebed's and her son Moses' story, you still can partner with God and find healthy options for your difficult decisions.

It's a Juggling Act

Tools for Choosing

When you're struggling with your new-mommy choices, whether big or small, consider the following tools that could help you gain clarity and understanding.

Ask Yourself

- What do I *really* want to do? What's my desired outcome?
- What additional knowledge do I need to have in order to make an informed decision?
- What resources are available to me?
- If you find yourself saying, "I don't have a choice," then ask yourself, "If I did have a choice, what would I do?" Then pause and listen for your spontaneous reply.

Flip a Coin Exercise

If you're having a tricky time deciding between two good choices, consider this quirky tool called the Flipped Coin Exercise explained in my book *The Relief of Imperfection*. When you have two choices that are reasonable and beneficial and it really doesn't matter which one is "just right," flip a coin. Before you toss it, choose your side. When you see which side it lands on, pay attention to how you *feel* about that choice. Happy it landed that way? A little disappointed? Now you know what you really wanted to do all along. Go for it! (Try this when you can't decide between two good possibilities in other areas of your life. Like which color car you want to buy. Or which Bible study you want to join. Or which outfit you want to wear for your next night out with your spouse. It'll make you smile and give you a break from trying too hard to make it all just right!)

Brainstorming in Color

At times you may be tempted to get stuck in all-or-nothing, black-and-white thinking. For example, if you discover that you need to return to work for financial reasons, instead of thinking it *must* be an 8:00 to 5:00, five-day-a-week job, explore other options such as part-time or freelance work or talk to your boss about telecommuting, compressing your work week, job sharing, or even taking your baby with you. I call this "thinking in color." I have several life coaching clients who choose their favorite color (one chose raspberry, another orange, still another deep ocean blue), and then visualize brainstorming options in that color when they're tempted to default to black-and-white thinking. Try it. It just might work for you, too.

[God] tends his flock like a shepherd:
He gathers the lambs in his arms
and carries them close to his heart;
he gently leads those that have young.

ISAIAH **40:11** NIV

Safe in God's Arms

Rocking Baby/Rocking Mom

A new mommy named Danielle who works a full-time job outside
the home wrote:

*I don't write poetry, but if I did I would wax eloquent about the
amazingness of rocking a baby. Everything is okay with my world when I'm
swaying in the chair with my baby girl.*

*Before I leave for work in the mornings and each evening when I return,
I sit down in the rocking chair and my baby and I relax together. The stress,
exhaustion, and sense of being overwhelmed melt away as I feel the full weight
of her trusting body against my heart, her chubby hand touching my arm,
and her hair caressing my face. Her familiar smell (I'd know it blindfolded)
lifts my spirits, and the many decisions I face pale in importance. This quiet
time that I spend nursing and rocking my baby grounds me and reminds me
of what really brings me joy.*

As Danielle shared her story, I closed my eyes and remembered
how it felt to rock Lynnette and Rich. Her experience mirrored mine.

It reminds me of God's gentle and loving care for you, Mom. How
He longs to gather you to His heart and hold you securely, all the while
assuring you that He loves you more than you'll ever know. When
your mind feels like it's going to burst with all the choices you must
make and tasks you must achieve, take a few moments to visualize Him
rocking you to sleep. And awakening you again, refreshed and ready to
follow His lead as you make the decisions you face.

*People who say they sleep like babies
usually don't have them.*

LEO J. BURKE

Chapter 4

Sleepless Nights/ Blurry Days

What's Up, Mom?

A Little Sleep Please

"It's still in the planning stage, but my husband and I are trying to work it out," announced my dental hygienist, Sarah. Having no clue where she was headed with this one-way conversation (her fingers filled my wide-open mouth), I speculated that she and her spouse were taking a cruise, buying a new house, or moving across the country.

"A little break—just to the motel down the street. I'll come home for an hour in the evening to nurse our baby. All I want to do is sleep till I wake up!"

Switching gears in mid-monologue, she mentioned her current dilemma: trying to find a babysitter for a staff meeting the next day. I listened and remembered. (Obviously, I was in no position to say anything, yet I tried to show a little empathy with my eyes.)

"I'm just so tired," she continued. "Sleepless nights. Blurry days. It's getting to me." The look in my eyes must have turned to alarm, since she quickly added, "Oh, don't worry, I've had several cups of coffee. You and your teeth will be fine."

Bedtime Stories and Earrings

Fatigue—it sits on your head like a box of bricks and makes moving through your regular daily activities feel like you're mired in quicksand. You're on heightened alert status around the clock (or so it seems), sleeping lightly so you can awaken to any unusual sounds from the baby. If you're like my dental hygienist, you've tried napping when the baby naps and catching snatches of sleep between working, cleaning, laundering, cooking, diapering, showering, and connecting with your friends, family, and spouse. But you're exhausted. You've tried to hide it behind the java jolts and makeup, but now everyone knows because you fell face-first into your dinner plate last night. Well, maybe not. But it could have happened. Yes?

Listening to Sarah's tales of new momhood reminded me of my own interrupted nights and foggy days. One particular sleep-deprived memory pops into my mind. Reading my little ones a bedtime story (a ritual I started with both of them just a few months after each one was born), I gathered them both in my arms and we cuddled together on the bed. Marching through one of their favorite books, I took a slight detour from the storyline.

"*Goodnight room. Goodnight moon. Goodnight cow jumping over the moon. Goodnight light, and the red balloon. . .*" Then I mumbled a line that author Margaret Wise Brown never wrote into her classic children's book, *Good Night, Moon*: "And I see the earrings on top of the bright green drawers."

It didn't rhyme. My body jerked, and I started chuckling when I realized what happened. I had fallen asleep in the middle of reading the book and immediately starting dreaming of jewelry and furniture. *Talk about a tired mommy!* I laugh at this story, but the sleep deprivation most new mothers experience (at least in the first few weeks or months) is no laughing matter.

Legally Impaired

According to Harvard Medical School professor Charles A. Czeister, someone who averages just four hours of sleep a night for four to five nights has the same mental impairment as a person who's legally drunk. *Yikes!* No wonder I felt like a walking zombie after almost two years of waking up several times a night with my adorable baby boy (who, by the way, I fell in love with the moment I fixed my eyes on him).

I know that not all new mothers experience such sleeplessness and resulting exhaustion. Recently I asked the following question on Facebook: "Did you have trouble with being tired, exhausted, or sleep-deprived when you were a new mom?"

"No," wrote Barbara. "I didn't have trouble with exhaustion when my son was a baby. Not sure why, but I slept better than ever even though I breastfed him once in the middle of the night. My mind and body just seemed to be running on love-love-love!" And Marilyn responded, "Not a big problem for me. I just napped when my babies napped and worked when they were awake. That philosophy worked for me *most* of the time."

But the rest of the respondents seemed to shout through cyberspace, *"Yes! Yes! Yes!"* Some agreed with Karen who posted: "Definitely! Much lack of sleep resulting in many blurry days, especially with my first one. I woke up at every little peep with both girls, but my husband slept through anything. I've never slept quite as soundly since. Even now, two decades later, I awaken easily at sounds. And to think that I used to be a very sound sleeper—in my life before kids!"

Rebecca says, "I'm there all the time! Exhausted and foggy, that is. Still I'm old enough to know that there is nothing else in the world that would make me so happy to be this tired over and over and over again!" Becca has given birth to two little boys—and is also foster mother to three other babies.

That Exhaustion Slide

Dr. Suzanne Griffin, MD, clinical assistant professor of psychiatry at Georgetown University Medical Center and a private practice psychiatrist in Chevy Chase, Maryland, writes, "Hormones can affect sleep, especially in high doses. Vasopressin and oxytocin are present in high levels during the postpartum period in both the mother and the infant. That's why a new mother's sleep rhythms are in sync with her baby. Hormones facilitate the coupling of mom and baby."[4]

So, new mom, I guess you can blame some of your sleeplessness and tired state on hormones. Yet, this is just one reason for disruptive sleep patterns. Foster mothers like Rebecca and even daddies can get in on the exhaustion slide—even without the elevation of the hormones related to post-pregnancy and breastfeeding.

Blessed to Exhaustion

Recently I read a fun article written by new daddy Allen Harris. "My bedtime and wake time are racing toward each other in some freakish game of chicken. However, there's no winner in this race; there's just a tragic crash in the middle." Harris's experiences are not

---

4 http://www.babyzone.com/mom_dad/womens_health/sleep_mom/article/sleep-cycles-mom-baby.

all that unusual according to many new fathers. Sleep deprivation, additional financial stress, concerns about their wife's welfare, and a major change in lifestyle can render sleepless nights and blurry days for dads, too.[5]

I think most new mothers and fathers can identify with Harris as he concluded, "My life today is radically different than the quiet, orderly one I maintained a little over a year ago. But the truth is, I absolutely love my life now. . . . I never knew that it was even possible to be blessed to the point of physical exhaustion. Catching the blessings overflowing from God's storehouse is hard work! And. . . I'm not about to ask God to stop sending His goodness my way."[6]

Your heavenly Father's love shines bright in the smiles, cries, and gurgles of your tiny baby. And Mommy, God enjoys sharing His brilliant newborn creativity with you. He knows you are tired from waking up in the middle of the night to comfort, feed, and change your baby.

God also knows that these relentless, exhausting nights and foggy days won't last forever. In the meantime, when you feel like you can't take another step, please know that He hears your sighs and wants to help you find a little relief. So let God know how you're feeling, ask Him for guidance, and watch for the surprising ways He attends to your needs. Because He *never* gets tired.

5 Allen Harris, "Blessed into Exhaustion: A Father's Whine," *In Touch*, (June 2010): 22–24.
6 Ibid.

The Lord is the everlasting God,
the Creator of the ends of the earth.
He will not grow tired or weary,
and his understanding no one can fathom.
He gives strength to the weary and increases the power
of the weak. Even youths grow tired and weary,
and young men stumble and fall;
but those who hope in the Lord will renew their
strength. They will soar on wings like eagles;
they will run and not grow weary,
they will walk and not be faint.

ISAIAH 40:28–31 NIV

Who, Me?

What's Your Reality?

"I'm pretty sure I'll never shave my legs, exfoliate my face, pluck my eyebrows, color my hair, dust the piano keys, read the paper *or* a devotional in peace again. I'm just pooped. They say I'm supposed to sleep when the baby sleeps. That would be in about thirty-minute increments by the time I feed her, clean her up, settle her down, get her back to sleep—and then relax enough to get some shut-eye myself," said my new-mom friend. "In the meantime, I might as well say *sayonara* to living a regular life. I sound like such a whiner. . . ."

So what's it like for you, Mom? What's your reality? Sometimes it helps to "see" what's really going on so you can be more specific about what to pray, how to ask others for help, and about finding practical ways to be gentle with yourself as well as your baby.

Making It Personal

To help you assess your current reality, scan the following questions and respond with the first thing that pops into your head, even though it might be a foggy thought! (This is *not* a test. It will not be graded!)

- When was your baby born? How many days or months has it been since your world changed forever?
- During those first few weeks after your baby's birth/arrival how often did you awaken each night to feed and tend to your new baby?

- What were your sleeping and resting patterns during your last trimester of pregnancy or before your baby came? Were you already tired when your baby arrived?
- How would you characterize your labor, delivery, and immediate postpartum?
- What kind of help and support did you have immediately after your baby was born?
- What kind of help and support do you have now?
- How would you describe your personality style? Spontaneous? Laid back? Intense? Organized? Conscientious? Outspoken? Extroverted? Introverted? Anxious? Easygoing?
- How many times were you awakened last night? The night before?
- When was the last time you had a couple hours to do something you enjoy—just for you?

Your Sleepy Conclusion and God's Reassurance

Now in the next one to two minutes, jot down how you feel about your spontaneous answers to these questions. One woman wrote, "Well, no wonder I'm so tired." Another shared her surprising thoughts: "My, I've had more active support and respite times than I thought. Time for me to be grateful and capitalize on what I already have." Still another realized that during her recent pregnancy and delivery she'd had several more complications than with her previous one, so she decided to reduce her ultrahigh expectations and give herself some time to recover.

What about you? What are your practicalities and realities right now? You *can* take care of yourself. Go ahead. God *wants* you to. In fact, in Proverbs, God's manual for wise living, are these words: "Above all else, guard your heart, for everything you do flows from it" (Proverbs 4:23 NIV).

At first glance it may seem that this Bible verse focuses primarily on encouraging you to protect and grow your spiritual life. And while doing so *is* vital, this wise principle of life encompasses more than that. After researching the meanings of the original language, we notice that "above all else" (first and foremost) you've been given the privilege and responsibility to protect, maintain, preserve, and "guard" (nurture) your self. In Old Testament times, the people acknowledged that the word *soul* encompassed your personality, feelings, mind, and body.

Mom, you have the opportunity to nourish and strengthen yourself so you can reach out to nourish and actively care for those you love, including your baby. Admittedly, this is often difficult to do when you're tired, overwhelmed and sleepless in *su casa*!

Gently Now

So take it slowly. What one thing can you do today to make it possible to get a little more sleep, relief, and rest? Maybe that one thing is just to gently remind yourself that these all-consuming-infant days won't last forever. Recently one new mom wrote me a message on Twitter: "I'm not the world's worst mom, I'm just new at this game. Once I realized that, I relaxed." Hopefully you can take a cue from this new mommy and give yourself a break, too.

Been There—Done That

Melinda Strives to Be Supermom

*When my long-awaited baby boy was born I wanted to be Supermom.
So I assured my husband that he didn't need to take off any time from
his busy work schedule. And I told my family that I'd be fine without
any extra help or overnight stays. Gathering my pregnancy and new-baby
books around me, I tackled this new life phase with the same gusto I'd
always done everything else in my life.*

*When my in-laws came in to town to see their new grandson, I
cooked everyone a big meal: meat, potatoes, gravy, vegetables, salad, rolls,
special appetizers, and coffee. I even baked made-from-scratch buttermilk
brownies for dessert. I was determined to do everything just right, yet
terrified I wouldn't.*

*I felt exhausted from all the late nights, interrupted sleep, and busy,
blurry days. Looking back now, I realize that my mind was just a tad bit
foggy. Oh, who am I kidding? I had mega trouble focusing, evidenced by
the fact that I took my prize brownies (baked in a glass pan) from the oven,
set them on a burner, turned on the heat, and left the kitchen to greet my
guests. I haven't a clue why I did this. Soon I heard a bubbling sound and
smelled burned chocolate wafting down the hall.*

*My sister-in-law (a nurse) saw the horrified look in my swollen eyes.
"Melinda, you're exhausted. Let me help you." She had watched me dash
to pick up the baby every time he whimpered, sprint back to the kitchen,
and repeat this scenario several times. "What's happening here?" she asked.*

"Looks like you're running yourself ragged."

"Just the regular stuff for new moms, I'm sure," I responded. "He needs me a lot."

She followed me into the nursery and asked me a few short questions. Is he hungry? (No.) Is he wet? (No.) Is he in pain? (No, don't think so.) Is he in danger? (No.) "Well honey, sometimes a baby just gets overstimulated and needs to fuss a bit before he finally relaxes and slips off to sleep. You know how he's been passed from person to person all evening. Let's just leave him alone to settle down for a little while."

To my shock, her strategy worked. So I tried it again and again. Soon he slept through the night—and so did I. My over-attentiveness actually kept both of us from getting the rest we needed. The excessive doing and over-helping wasn't really helping. Imagine that!

Adjusting Unrealistic Expectations

Perhaps you identify with Melinda. Perhaps not. In either case, it's a relief to know that God doesn't expect you to do it all just right, all the time without pausing to refuel. You don't have to have five-course meals, spotless floors, or the bed made every day. You can relax your unrealistic expectations while you get accustomed to this new-mommy career.

God loves to give rest and restorative sleep to His children—and that includes you and your baby.

*It is in vain that you rise up early
and go late to rest, eating the bread of
anxious toil; for he gives sleep to his beloved.*
PSALM **127:2** NRSV

Here's an idea, tired mommy. Jot the words of Psalm 127:2 on a sticky note or 3 x 5 card and put it where you can see and read it often. Turn this verse into a prayer and pray it when you're overanxious or worn-out. Perhaps something like:

Lord, I want to relax and enjoy my role as a new mom. Please help me. I release my worries about how to get everything done to You. Calm my mind and help me to get the restorative sleep I need to care for my baby, myself, and my family. Lead me to others who are willing to help. Thank You for Your constant and understanding love. Amen.

Getaway Backfire

After our son was born, my husband sent me on an overnight getaway to a hotel in the mountains. Because I was nursing, I took along six-week-old Rich. That was the plan. Daddy Richard knew I was exhausted from waking up so many times each night with the baby, running after our three-year-old daughter, helping with the teens at church, and keeping the proverbial home fires burning.

It was a nice gesture on my husband's part, and since I hadn't told him what I needed (daily help/support so I could get frequent little naps, a listening ear, validation that I was doing an okay job, and help with meals), it was his way of saying, "I care."

Yet sadly, I became so concerned (okay, anxious!) that I please him, appear grateful, and do the getaway *just right* that my muscles tensed, my mind raced, and my ears over-sensitized listening for a baby-cry that wasn't even there. I didn't sleep a wink. Nada! *Bummer.*

I wish I would have shared my needs a little more openly. I might have been able to relax and get more sleep if I had. So take a tip from the experiences of Melinda and me. If the way you've been attempting to "do" your new mommyhood hasn't been working that well, try a different tactic.

Remember that whenever anyone starts a new career, there is a steep learning curve. And by the way, if what you've been doing *is* working and you're getting good rest and gaining strength, keep it up.

It's a Juggling Act

Sleepless in Su Casa?

No doubt about it: Balancing self-care with other-care is some major juggling (not just the standard juggling with three balls, but the spectacular juggling act with fire, swords, and chairs!). There's just so much to discover, learn, and decide.

There's an abundance of advice (often conflicting) on the Internet and television, in magazines and books, from friends, family, and strangers. As one new mommy said, "New-motherhood and baby-care resources and ideas are helpful, but over-information can be annoying."

So here are a few ideas for relieving your sleepless nights and blurry days. Try what sounds like it might work. After giving it some time, if it doesn't work, toss it out. You're in charge!

1. Ask for what you need.

Be specific. Yet at the same time, acknowledge that other people have the right to say yes, no, "I'll think about it and get back to you," or to negotiate. If you don't verbalize what would actually help you, then your loved ones and even the medical community may insist on helping in a way that is actually not as beneficial as you would like.

For example, you may get surprised with a party or get-together that you don't want (especially if you're an introvert), or you might get too much "alone" time and not enough fun breaks (a downer if you're an extrovert.) If you don't speak up and say you just want take-out for dinner, someone might whisk you to a restaurant when you're too tired to comb your hair or put on lip gloss. Or someone might plan a nice getaway for you when you're not ready yet!

2. Adjust your schedule to work for you now. You can readjust it later.

One mom found she tried too hard to push her baby into a four-hour feeding schedule—and it wore her out. She backed off and then was able to relax and sleep when her baby did. Another mom fed her baby every time he cried and that got to be too much, so she stretched her baby's schedule to at least two-hour feeding intervals.

Do what works for you. Someone is going to criticize you no matter what. If "before-baby" you always awakened at 5:30 a.m. to get going by 7:00, it is okay for you to stay in bed and sleep a little longer while you and baby are adjusting.

3. Involve your husband.

One husband said, "Carol takes care of all the baby's needs while I'm at work during the day, so I figure I can at least get up a few nights a week to change his diaper and bring him to her to nurse him in bed. Hopefully, she'll stay groggy enough to easily drift back to sleep."

Another hubby put the basinet on his side of the bed. When the baby started to whimper and it wasn't feeding time, he just jiggled the basinet, rocking him back to sleep. It worked for them. Mom got a little extra sleep.

4. Get help.

When you have other babies or preschoolers at home, the admonition to "nap when baby naps" can seem like a bad joke. So think outside the box. Is there a toddler community class she can attend? A Mom's Morning Out at the corner church?

Can your toddler go on a play-date with another family for a couple hours? Maybe someone can pick up your preschooler to take her to the mall or park while you crawl back into bed for a few more winks while the baby sleeps.

If you have the financial resources, consider hiring a postpartum doula. Europeans have used this option successfully for years. It works especially well if you've had a C-section and are not allowed to lift or drive.

Also, don't be reluctant to ask your mom, sister, aunt, or grandma to come stay with you for a while. For some reason new moms think they can do it all on their own and are bent on proving it (remember Melinda's story?). But it's okay. *Really.* No matter what you think your husband or your family expects of you. Let others do the laundry, cooking, cleaning, and answering the phone. You sleep.

Practical Tips for Reducing Sleep Deprivation

- Put up room-darkening shades or curtains (before you come home from the hospital).
- Try nursing your baby in bed instead of sitting in a chair. Fall back to sleep together. (Many times babies don't need burping when they nurse this way.)
- Have a cup of chamomile tea while nursing or before bedtime.
- Put the baby's receiving blanket in the dryer for a quick warm up. Maybe she'll sleep longer so you can, too. (Try this for your blanket or afghan, too.)

- Use a sound machine for baby (or for yourself).
- Keep baby near your bed in a basinet or co-sleeper for the first few weeks.
- Put a twin-size bed in the nursery, and sleep there when you're extra tired.
- Take a hot shower or bath before going to bed in the evening. No, you don't have to wash and style your hair!
- Refrain from working on the computer or watching an intense movie right before trying to sleep.
- When you're too wired to sleep, tell yourself, *It's okay, I'll sleep later*, instead of berating yourself with *I should be asleep; what's wrong with me?*
- Take four long, slow breaths in and out while you're lying in bed.
- Every day eat something with protein in it, or you might get too worn out to rest well.
- Listen to your favorite soothing music before going to sleep.
- Send Spot away for a week or two so you can sleep instead of taking care of the dog.
- Order takeout so you can take a catnap instead of cooking.
- Turn off your cell phone so the ring won't wake you up while you're trying to nap. (Check texts and e-mails occasionally and not continually.)

Safe in God's Arms

What's Up, Lord?

Sleep! We crave it when we're exhausted. Yet it often doesn't come easily. We resent it when we're busy and think we don't have time for it. When we ignore it, it threatens to derail us. And when we try too hard to hurry up and capture it, it runs away. Ironically, the bottom-line remains: We need it to stay alive and thrive. Sleep! It's one of the constant push-pull anomalies in our current bigger-better-faster culture.

Add a helpless newborn baby depending on you 24–7, and sleep becomes more elusive than you ever thought possible. You get more tired than you ever imagined you'd be, longing for sleep like you never thought you would—or could.

What exactly was God thinking when He created sleep? He could have chosen a different way to sustain and revitalize His children. But He didn't. He gives us the gift of sleep—and then seems to inexplicably withdraw it when we become new mommies. *So what's up, Lord?*

According to polls, statistics, conversations, and stories, sleeplessness remains a key difficulty for new moms. I think God knows that. After all, He created you—and your baby. He cares about what's going on with you and what you're feeling and facing. And although there are steps you can take to help yourself, new mom, the reality is: Your sleep will be broken while your baby is getting accustomed to living in this world. As it has for other mothers, perhaps these words from Isaiah will help you, too.

Mom, lift up your hand toward God. He is reaching down to you. He'll take hold of your hand and guide you through these rough months. They won't last forever. But *He* will.

The Lᴏʀᴅ made the earth and everything that grows on it. He gives breath to its people. He gives life to those who walk on it. He says to his servant, "I, the Lord, have chosen you to do what is right. I will take hold of your hand. I will keep you safe."

Iꜱᴀɪᴀʜ 42:5–6 NIʀᴠ

Many waters cannot quench love;
rivers cannot sweep it away.
Song of Solomon 8:7 NIV

Chapter 5

What Ever Happened to Romance?

What's Up, Mom?

Not so good?

"How's it going at home?" I overheard Lucille, our senior pastor's wife, ask my husband, Richard, a few weeks after our first child was born. Just four months before, we had moved 1,300 miles across the country from Kansas City, Kansas, to Bakersfield, California, so that Richard could serve as youth pastor at a large West Coast church.

Hmmmm. I wonder how he's going to respond to that one. I strained to hear his answer.

"Well, sometimes it's fine and at other times, it's not so good," said my normally elusive husband.

"It's so refreshing to hear that." Then she laughed a little too robustly—or so I thought! *What was so hilarious about the fact that things at home were "not so good" at times?* Then she continued: "And isn't that the truth with a newborn, especially the first one. Many won't admit it, though. I love your authenticity, dad."

Doing Marriage after Childbirth

New mom, having a baby upends your world, that's for sure. Your hormones whirl inside you, sleep avoids you, the learning curve overwhelms you, and as your brain fogs up Ole Lady Exhaustion becomes an unwanted roommate. You hurt from the labor and delivery. And well, everything is just so new. Yet you're not the only one who is swimming—and sometimes going under for the third time—in a murky unknown ocean (figuratively speaking, of course). Your baby's father is thrashing around in this new world, too.

A young couple recently told me to "write an entire chapter on marriage after childbirth. If other new moms and dads are anything like us, then there are a lot of malnourished couples out there who need a little—or rather mega-much!—help, love, and understanding." They continued to explain what they meant with this impromptu dialogue:

Husband: I didn't know what to do.

Wife: I was a new mommy, and since giving birth is a natural act, we both thought I'd surely know what to do. But most of the time, I simply didn't have a clue.

Husband: Then most bewildering of all was the fact that she couldn't seem to figure out what she wanted. I tried to help. Then she cried, and I automatically thought I was doing something wrong—or that she was mad at me. Or worse, that she (my beloved wife and the mommy of my new heir!) didn't love me anymore.

Wife: Parenting is not always the pretty, affectionate picture that books, magazines, and Mother's Day sermons lead you to believe it will be.

Who Knew?

Backing up this young couple's story is another one shared by a handsome young daddy:

After our first son was born and my wife and he came home from the hospital, I set them up in our bedroom. I gathered all the baby's necessities and placed them within her reach, added flowers, juice, and background music. I held her hand, kissed her on the forehead, and I assured her that I'd be glad to help with whatever she needed. And then she yelled, "Get out of here!"

So I did. I went golfing.

When I returned, she greeted me at the door and sobbed out these words, "Why'd you leave? I needed you."

Who knew? Certainly not me. I genuinely thought she wanted to be alone with the baby. After all, she told me in no uncertain terms to "go away."

Discombobulated

When Baby comes and makes your comfortable (and amorous) twosome an uncomfortable (and distant) threesome, life gets discombobulated. All that you thought you knew about love, romance, the marriage relationship, and working together comes into question. And the truth is, your life together as a couple will never be quite the same. You're in the midst of a major life change that can sometimes trigger old fears, insecurities, and past painful experiences.

Maybe you long for a few quiet moments alone together, just the two of you enjoying one another's company like *before*. Or perhaps you haven't even had the time or energy to think about it. In either case, the reality remains that those kind of moments are rare to nonexistent in the first few weeks and months of parenthood. Nothing squashes romance like a screeching baby or a smelly diaper needing to be changed in the middle of a candlelight dinner or heart-to-heart chat.

Mommy's Viewpoint

Your life now includes many practicalities and realities that make it difficult to connect romantically—or in any other meaningful way—with your baby's daddy. Okay, that's an understatement. Your hormones seem to have betrayed you, and perhaps they have. Libido can be quite low while you're breastfeeding and getting your chemicals back to normal.

Not only that, you're exhausted, confused, and often in pain. The baby needs you 24-7; and although he is adorable (the baby, not necessarily your husband!) you're tired of giving your mind and body to another human being, even one who is merely a few days or months old. You just want a little space.

Daddy's Viewpoint

As for daddy, he now carries pictures where his money used to be— and he feels the financial pressure. He's pooped, even though it may be apparent that he gets more sleep than Mommy does. He says he's tired of maneuvering around all the new baby toys, supplies, and equipment that are scattered throughout your bedroom and the rest of the house. And he doesn't seem to "get it" that Mom has little (okay, perhaps zero) time, energy, or interest in organizing it all— or merely picking up.

When they're away, most husbands seem genuinely concerned about their wives and the baby. Recently a new daddy confided to me, "The hardest thing I had to do after our daughter was born was go back to work. I didn't know how to express it, but I did worry that my wife was getting so worn out."

Daddy may even be a tad bit envious of all the attention the baby gets from the woman he married. One young father asked his seasoned, older Bible-study mentor, "When will my loving and attentive wife come back?"

"Well, if I remember correctly, it will happen about the time your youngest child goes off to college and then you'll be faced with an entirely different issue: your wife's sadness at her empty nest," responded his mentor-friend, only a little tongue-in-cheek.

God's Viewpoint

This reality is enough to drive a couple into opposing corners with no visual way to come together even to shake hands. Did God know this was going to happen when He created the family, procreation, and parenthood?

Yes, I suppose He did, since He knows everything about everyone from the beginning of creation until this precise moment. He designed man and woman and said, *"This is good!"* And He'll continue to know all things when time as we know it ceases to be and He rules over a new heaven and earth.

There, as believers in Christ, we will live worry free. Sounds good, doesn't it? "But God made a promise to us. And we are waiting for what he promised—a new heaven and a new earth where goodness lives" (2 Peter 3:13 NCV). Still that's not happening yet.

This mom-dad relationship standoff wasn't in God's original design for men and women. Yet He foresaw what would happen when Adam and Eve pushed away from His guidelines and tried to be equal with their Maker. (Read Genesis 3:1–24.) Yes, God knows all things at all times. He's *omniscient,* which the dictionary defines as having infinite knowledge or understanding.

God Is Bigger

In case you're wondering, new mom, this *is* a good thing. Your loving Creator sees all that's going on inside you and around you. He isn't put off by your neediness, your humanness, or your struggles. In fact, He cares about you, your baby, and your relationships more than you'll ever understand. I hope this gives you reassurance and peace whether you're feeling pleased and grateful in your circumstances, overwhelmed by your reality, or disappointed in your own or someone else's behavior.

God is bigger than any of your wonderings (or wanderings)! He hears your heart and sees you, your baby, and your mate at all times—loving you through and in it all.

*This is the way we know that we belong
to the way of truth. When our hearts make
us feel guilty, we can still have peace before God.
God is greater than our hearts,
and he knows everything.*
1 JOHN 3:19–20 NCV

Who, Me?

Traditional or Not?

Throughout history, women of various ages, nationalities, backgrounds, religions, and potential have given birth to babies. Still others have chosen to adopt, love, nurture, and raise a child that someone else brought into the world. Not every mother is married or healthy or happy, yet some moms are all three.

Maybe you're in a traditional family situation (husband, wife, baby or babies). Maybe you're not. Either way, you're a valuable person, a woman God loves, and with whom He wants to develop a growing personal relationship. The apostle Paul makes this clear in the prayer he wrote in Ephesians 1:17 (NIV): "I keep asking that the God of our Lord Jesus Christ, the glorious Father, may give you the Spirit of wisdom and revelation, so that you may know him better."

If you're holding this book in your hands and skimming the pages, you're probably a new mom, have been one, or care deeply about one. If you're interested in this chapter's topic of "Whatever Happened to Romance?" and you're reading these words, chances are that you're married or thinking or dreaming about getting married. This might not be the case, but for the sake of this "romance" theme, we'll assume that you're interested in the world of husbands and wives.

Making It Personal

Even the lives of new moms who are married vary greatly. Some become mommies as teenagers. Others start their mother roles in their twenties or thirties. Some women wait to have their first child until they're in their forties or fifties. Where do you fit in this demographic?

Awareness is an important factor in building your self-confidence as a wife and mother. So in order to gain clarity about your specific situation, skim through the following questions. Jot your responses in the margins of this page, in your journal, in your mind, or not at all. Any way you decide to respond is fine.

- Did you have your baby within the first year of your marriage or did you wait a little longer?
- As a little girl did you dream of becoming a mother or were you ambivalent or undecided about having children?
- What kind of mother and/or father role models did you have as a child? Were either of your own parents rigid, shaming, or abusive?
- In your marriage, do you feel free to voice your thoughts, feelings, and perceptions or do you sometimes feel squashed or discounted?
- What do you enjoy about being a mother? What surprises you?
- In what way do you appreciate your husband in his new role as "daddy"?

- What would you like to tell your husband about your needs, wants, desires, and current feelings and thoughts?

When you want to grow or change your life in any area (emotionally, mentally, physically, relationally, or spiritually), it is helpful to know more about yourself and your realities so that you can make intentional choices about your next action steps. Even when you're feeling tired and overwhelmed, you can make subtle changes that help you enjoy more satisfaction and grace in your family roles.

Ask God for Insight

Small awareness-insights are enough for now. As you read the stories and experiences of other moms and dads in this chapter (and the other sections of the book) highlight the quotes or ideas that impress you for any reason. Then ask God for deepened understanding. It's His joy to give you insight and wisdom in your journey as a wife and mother.

The LORD grants wisdom! From his mouth come knowledge and understanding. He grants a treasure of common sense to the honest.

PROVERBS 2:6–7 NLT

Been There—Done That

Daddy Can Do It, Too

Not every loving family has the traditional situation where dad works in an office and comes home each evening while mom stays at home to care for the baby. A few weeks ago I flew from Phoenix to Kansas City for my niece's wedding. Since I purchased my ticket from an airline with open seating, I needed to go online and get my boarding pass twenty-four hours ahead of time. But I forgot and consequently was the last one to board. Once on the plane I noticed the only seat left was next to a young couple with a tiny baby. This didn't bother me—a grandmother of seven—so I sat down and settled in.

The baby didn't cry once; and after a couple hours in the air, the mother excused herself to walk back to the restroom. While she was gone, the young father and I struck up a conversation. "How old is your little one?" I asked.

"Hank is three months old today."

We chatted a little while longer and then I said, "I'm writing a book for new moms, and I appreciate getting the input of parents who're navigating parenthood for the first time. How would you describe the hardest adjustment you faced after Hank was born?"

With no hesitation, he replied, "The sleeplessness. Definitely. We just got so tired. He didn't sleep much and cried when he was awake. I kept asking him, 'Well, what's wrong with you, son? I just fed you, changed you, rocked you.' Of course he didn't answer. I had to try to guess what he needed. It's confusing. But then one day he smiled at me—and everything changed. It got easier once he could smile back at me and we could interact."

"Sounds like you and your son have formed a special bond."

"Yes, we have. It was hard to schedule it all at first. He took a little formula, but mostly I gave him a bottle filled with his mother's milk. She's an emergency room doctor at a hospital in Portland, and her schedule varies. I stay home with Hank, so we don't need daycare. I used to work at the hospital, too. But even before my wife got pregnant, we decided she'd keep her position and I'd be with the baby."

"Well, congratulations for finding ways to make it all work for you. I can only imagine how busy you both are. Where are you headed on this trip?"

"We're visiting Grandma."

"Is this the first time she's seen him?"

"No. She came to Portland to visit us when he was six weeks old. My wife and I wanted to go cross-country skiing. To get to be alone, just the two of us. We didn't know if Grandma Helen would go for that, since he cried so much and all."

" 'You go,' she said. 'Don't worry about him. We'll be just fine.' "

" 'Oh, we're not worried,' we said in unison as the front door hit our backsides. We were so out of there! It was our first time to get a break and be together one-on-one; to have a little fun and connect as husband and wife. But it was also our last time. We still haven't felt comfortable hiring an unknown babysitter. You know what I mean?"

It Takes Two to Tango

That same week I received an e-mail from another new mom who worked part-time as the president of her growing young company. She wrote, "I just could not do the daily parenting dance alone. It definitely takes two to tango! I know moms who love and raise their babies by themselves quite successfully, and I guess I would figure it out if I had to. Yet I'm grateful I don't have to tackle this massive endeavor alone. It's more fun and makes the hard days a little less of a struggle because I have Matt in this with me."

Yet not all new moms experience this level of partnership with their spouses. While recently interacting with a group of talented and caring mothers I asked, "As a new mom, how did you and your husband find ways to connect?"

Melody said, "Sorry, can't give you a good answer about this. My husband was always gone working. I felt like I raised our three babies alone. I coped by sleeping when they did and praying a lot. But we're still together, and he's a great father now."

When Protecting Yourself and Your Baby Means Going It Solo

At first Barbara Jean simply said, "The truth is, it isn't always possible to connect. I tried. But I couldn't make it work, even though I wanted to. I got peace when I finally accepted my reality." Later Barbara shared a little more about her story:

If I can help another new mom, I'm willing. Maybe someone is walking in shoes similar to mine.

My husband left me emotionally and spiritually on the day we were married. I endured years of verbal and emotional threats and punishment. For what? I had no idea. When I got pregnant, the abuse escalated, and he punched me. He told me repeatedly that it was all my fault, and God was going to hound me for the rest of my life. This all stunned me since we were both Christians, active in our church, and had talked about having children.

I wanted to connect with him, yet he lived in a reality that was vastly different from mine or anyone else's. I feared for my life and felt guilty for failing God; yet I finally realized that I had a responsibility to protect myself and my unborn child. In accepting my reality, I was able to connect with caring people who helped me stay accountable. God became my source of peace. With a broken heart and deep love for my child, I kept moving forward toward freedom.

Getting Help Is Good with God

Although Barbara Jean would readily admit that raising her son as a single parent was not in her original plan, she made the decision to leave in order to protect herself and her child from danger—physical, emotional, and spiritual. The fact that abuse happens in marriages and often escalates after pregnancy remains a sobering reality.

It's not a lighthearted topic. Yet if you experience mistreatment like Barbara Jean did, please ask God to give you the courage you need to get help.

The Unspoken Connection

Judith was in that same group of moms I chatted with about the reconnection of mothers and fathers "after baby." She experienced a vastly different situation that some of you may identify with.

First of all, there was a surprising new connection that we shared. This awesome experience of becoming new parents together. Although it remained unspoken between us, we had an understanding. I remember Jon saying that he couldn't wait to come home for lunch to see the baby. That made my mommy-heart sing.

Still it was difficult. Neither of us performed perfectly in our new parenting partnership. As I look back I wish I would have communicated more about how I felt and what I needed. I think offering grace to one another was one of the best gifts we gave to each other. We didn't put a lot of words around any of this. But being imperfectly graceful toward one another in a completely unfamiliar territory was the thing that kept us going.

The Intentional Connection

Another mom talked of the practical steps she and her husband took to make sure they had time for one another:

After a few harried weeks, we agreed to spend some time sitting together at night after the babies were in bed. We talk, watch a movie, read, enjoy a snack. Sometimes we get creative and do a more energetic activity.

We feel this together-time is more important than getting the chores done. Since our youngest is still tiny and we don't have family close to babysit, we don't get to go out on dates right now. So we place high priority on this time together. It keeps us on the same page.

There's a Push/Pull

But it's not always smooth sailing for moms and dads when they try to navigate the new-parenting waters. Sometimes there's a push/pull going on between the husband and wife, like between Denae and her spouse:

I couldn't believe how incompetent I felt about my new mothering role. I had dreamed, prayed, and planned for this day since I was a little girl playing with my dolls. It did not help when my husband could calm my daughter better than I could. I was the one who was supposed to know exactly what to do. Not him. How dare he?

After a while I did learn to appreciate his involvement. Now three babies later, I still have insecurities—and I'm grateful for Brandon's help.

However, parenting experts agree that in many cases, the new father is the one who feels left out—or irrelevant. Picture this scenario. Daddy comes in the door, hunts for his new baby, picks her up, looks into her eyes, and makes funny faces. Baby starts to cry. Daddy rocks Baby back and forth, trying to comfort her. Baby starts to wail. Mom runs in and takes Baby. Baby calms. Screeching stops. Mom starts to nurse Baby. Daddy slinks into another room. *What good am I?* he thinks. *Guess they don't need me.*

Hardwired

For men who are hardwired (it's in their brain chemistry) to find solutions and fix dilemmas (to be needed), it's quite uncomfortable to feel helpless. After all, he may have experienced powerlessness during his wife's labor. That wasn't cool. Now here he is again—surprised by his negative thoughts and emotions.

He might find he's a tinge jealous of the attention and time his wife gives to the baby. Statistics indicate that as many as 14 percent of new dads even get postpartum depression similar to moms. Yet Daddy may not acknowledge or admit to having these strange feelings, so he just gets grumpy. Becoming irritable is easier for him to handle.

It's a Juggling Act

What to Do?

So what's a tired, sore, hormonally challenged new mommy to do? How can she help herself and her baby while reconnecting to her husband at a time when she can barely walk and hold her eyes open? The solutions may not come automatically, even though she loves him dearly.

Nurturing your relationship during this transitional time in your marriage takes intentionality on the part of two maturing (although not perfect) adults. You can't change his personality, values, or beliefs. Only he and God can do that. (Hey, you're off the hook. Isn't that a relief?)

Yet you can be yourself, share your own genuine needs and desires, and take responsibility for your own health, emotional growth, and spiritual development. You're only one-half of this husband-wife/mom-dad partnership, it's true. Yet you can do your part. Skim through the following ideas and choose one that sounds doable to you.

1. Relax and take care of yourself.

As a sleep-deprived new mom, you may simply not have much energy to put forth the effort to interact with your husband. Also you may be feeling unattractive if you have bags under your eyes, stretch marks, or extra baby-pounds. Give yourself a break.

As soon as it's feasible, plan to do some intentionally relaxing self-care activities, such as scheduling and enjoying a massage in your home or at a nearby salon or spa. (Ask your husband, a relative, or close trusted friend to watch the baby for an hour or so.)

Take a catnap whenever you can.

Light a fragrant candle (lavender, chamomile, and sandalwood are relaxing scents) while you're nursing or giving the baby her bottle.

If your husband complains or questions your decision to rest instead of cleaning the bathtub or loading the dishwasher, explain that it's important to you—and him. In a calm tone, tell him that you just can't continue to try to do it all and still stay relaxed for time with him.

2. Ask.

You've probably heard it before, but here it is again: Husbands cannot read your mind. *Oh, but if he really loved me, he would figure out what I need, wouldn't he?* Uhhh. Not really.

One experienced mommy of a thirteen-month-old told her weepy sister-in-law with a two-week-old to explicitly ask her husband for what she needed. So one frustrating afternoon when weepy mom felt like she couldn't go on and her exasperated husband didn't know what to do, she took her sister-in-law's advice. "I want a *People* magazine, a tall Coke, and a nap," she said clearly and calmly. "Well, okay then," said her husband. And soon mom had all three.

3. Express gratitude.

Your man is a problem-solver. In the midst of a dilemma, he wants to know that he can make a positive difference. Yet often during your pregnancy, labor, delivery, and postpartum, he may wonder if his presence even matters.

If you appreciated his presence in the labor and delivery room, tell him so. Let him know you're grateful when he helps with the baby, makes a sandwich, goes to the store, pays the bills, gives your older child a bath, or listens to you tell about your frustrating experience at the doctor's office.

4. Include Dad in Baby's care.

Experience reveals that many fathers don't bond with their babies until they turn one year old. This is usually when baby starts walking and is able to greet him with upheld arms and laughter. Then Daddy begins to see the personality that Mom has enjoyed for months.

One young mom said, "I loved it when my husband and our firstborn spent time together, but it didn't happen very often. I decided to help them connect. He had a flexible job, so I called him sometimes to ask him to drop by the house between 9:30 and 10:30 a.m., knowing that this would be her most active time. Then I'd put her in his arms and tell him what to say and do to bring on her giggles. He loved it, and so did she."

Another new daddy said, "Instead of continuing to feel left out when she nursed our son, I asked my wife to let me know what rituals and routines I *could* do."

5. Pray for your husband.

While you're praying for yourself, your baby, and your friends, also pray for your husband. Move beyond prayers that "he will wake up and be nicer to me." (Okay, maybe you've never asked God for anything like that!) Pray that God will bless him and guide him in his work, relationships, and spiritual life.

Consider using a Bible prayer as a guide as you pray for the man you fell in love with and married and who became the daddy of your baby. Janice used Ephesians 3:16–19 as a framework in praying for her husband, Bill. (Use any Bible translation or paraphrase that you have and substitute the word *you* with your husband's name.)

Here's an example of how Janice prayed: "Lord, I pray that out of [Your] glorious riches [You] may strengthen [Bill] with power through [Your] Spirit in [his] inner being, so that Christ may dwell in [his heart] through faith. And I pray that [Bill], being rooted and established in love, may have power, together with all the saints, to grasp how wide and long and high and deep is the love of Christ, and to know this love that surpasses knowledge—that [Bill] may be filled to the measure of all the fullness of God" (based on Ephesians 3:16–19 NIV).

6. Empathize.

Daddy gets tired, fed up, and discouraged, too. This parenting gig feels as new and overwhelming to him as it does to you. Just the other day, an involved young father of three little ones shared his new-daddy frustration during an interview with me. "I don't want to sound like a bad dad. You know I care. But I'm just done, worn out. It's a huge strain to constantly deal with crying, diapers, sleeplessness, juggling, working, marriage, and all the financial pressure." Let your husband know that you realize this is a difficult adjustment for him, also.

Your husband is experiencing new feelings about you, Mom. Before you got pregnant and delivered his child, he thought of you as his wife, companion, and lover. Now he may have been in the labor room and/or delivery room. He saw you endure the pain and now sees you manage the baby. He's probably amazed at your courage and strength; and he's in the process of integrating his memory of you from before with the person you displayed during labor-delivery and who you are now.

Accept his sincere apologies and trust his honest sharing—even if it doesn't happen often enough in your estimation. One woman said that her husband apologized for not being understanding and attentive to her needs. Then he added, "I'm determined to treat you better, but I won't do it perfectly. Please be patient with me."

Understand that the wait to make love again while you're healing from the childbirth is genuinely difficult for your husband.

7. Communicate.

Each member of your family (mom, dad, baby—and any older children) may be a little confused and uncertain during this transition. Your most effective relationship tool at this time is communication. Easier said than done, yes! When your husband shares his thoughts and feelings with you, refrain from trying to fix him with Bible verses or advice. (Of course, you want him to do the same for you. So consider telling him that.)

Your husband may be wondering when you'll be ready to resume lovemaking. Although it's often difficult for women to understand, the fact remains that men show and experience their feelings of love and intimacy through the act of sexual intercourse. He might not verbalize it, but it's quite possible that he's worried about whether you still love him, find him attractive, and want to be sexually intimate with him.

Typical medical recommendations include waiting six weeks before resuming vaginal sex after childbirth. Sometimes it's longer. And since some women have a difficult time during pregnancy, necessitating sexual abstinence then as well, it may have been awhile since hubby enjoyed sex with you. (Okay, admittedly it seems like forever to him!) Assuring him of your love while communicating the reasons for the wait (and your low libido) might help him cope. Consider calmly explaining the following:

- Lochia: Go ahead and educate your husband about this normal vaginal discharge. It might prove to be a useful anti-aphrodisiac!
- Vaginal soreness/episiotomy/perineal tearing/C-section: It's been said that helping someone identify and *feel* what you're trying to convey will cause them to better understand your message. Help your husband appreciate the extent of your vaginal soreness by suggesting that he describe what it was like when he got hit hard in the groin. Ask, "How long did the contact last?" and "How long were you in pain?" As he's wincing, ask if he remembers how long you were in labor and delivery. *Hmmmm.* If you're recovering from a C-section or long episiotomy, you might share with him that even sneezing, urination, and having a bowel movement causes pain.
- Hormone fluctuation: If you're breastfeeding, medical

researchers agree that your sex drive dips with your lowered
estrogen levels. Also some moms don't like it when they leak
milk during sex.

Of course, being on call for your baby 24–7 and feeling more
exhausted than you ever thought possible doesn't help either. Even
though it may be difficult, endeavor to be upfront about your
physical and emotional discomfort. And assure both yourself and
your husband that these conditions won't last forever.

8. Plan for together time.

As soon as possible, ask a trusted relative or close friend to watch
the baby for a couple hours while you go on a date. Although your
first few short getaways might not be your fantasy date, try to accept
what you have at the moment. Laugh, listen, hug, and touch while
you're on this short adventure together, even though you may be
groggy, tired, and preoccupied with thoughts of the baby.

9. Get help if needed.

According to recent research, both new mothers and new fathers
can experience postpartum depression. Also, many mental health
experts maintain that past hurtful experiences in childhood can be
triggered when we have our own children. You and/or your spouse
may benefit from counseling if you're at a complete standstill in your
relationship.

Dr. Bill Sears of the well-respected family of experts in pediatric
medicine writes, "I have never seen a case of mother burnout in a
family where the father is actively involved in parenting and in caring

for the new mother. Some dads are good at this right from the start. Others need encouragement. Mother[s] can help their husbands by stating clearly and calmly what her own needs are."[7]

Parents can experience burnout in their work or relationship. Understanding the definition of *burnout* may be helpful in determining the help that you or your spouse need. Burnout is "the type of stress and emotional fatigue, frustration, and exhaustion that occurs when a series of (or combination of) events in a relationship, mission, way of life, or job fail to produce an expected result."[8] If either of you struggle with depression or burnout after the birth of your child, you may have difficulty communicating your thoughts, emotions, or needs to one another. It's not a weakness to seek help. In fact, it shows maturity.

---

7 "Avoiding Mommy Burnout," AskDr.Sears.com, accessed 2006, http://www.askdrsears.com/html/10/t107600.asp.

8 Myron Rush, *Burnout* (Colorado Springs, Colorado: Victor Books, 1987), p. 13.

Safe in God's Arms

Help for Your Heart

I just hung up the phone with a young mom who told me about her recent lunch with several college friends. Now married, each young woman said the same thing: "We want to have a baby, but we're wondering if it's worth it. Every couple we know got divorced soon after they started having kids. It's scary."

Bringing a baby into your home does change the relationship you have with your husband, no doubt about it. You may grieve the loss of the old way. At the same time, you'll be making new memories and connections with the man you've chosen to share your life with. God designed families and He gives grace to help you as you walk down this bumpy parenthood road together.

We've discussed some of the marriage bumps in this chapter. You may question if God cares that you keep stepping on big rocks and in potholes that twist your ankle—and your heart. It hurts.

Does God care? Yes! He cares that you're confused about how to reconnect with your husband and that you ache about not being understood. "The LORD is close to the brokenhearted and saves those who are crushed in spirit" (Psalm 34:18 NIV).

Growing Up with God

God is not mad at you. He loves you. And your husband. And your baby. And your other children. He wants to free you to enjoy your life with your husband. "With God's power working in [you], God can do much, much more than anything [you] can ask or imagine" (Ephesians 3:20 NCV).

Your dreams, your hurts, your daily cares, and your family are safe with God. Hand over yourself, your husband, and your baby to Jesus. He'll help you become the mature woman He designed you to be and give you the strength and courage to share honestly with the man you fell in love with and married.

God wants us to grow up,
to know the whole truth and tell it in love—
like Christ in everything. We take our lead from
Christ, who is the source of everything we do.
He keeps us in step with each other. His very breath
and blood flow through us, nourishing us so that
we will grow up healthy in God, robust in love.

EPHESIANS 4:15 MSG

You know you're a mom when you say at least once a day, "I'm not cut out for this job," but you know you wouldn't trade it for anything.

UNKNOWN

Chapter 6

Who Hijacked My Body and Emotions?

What's Up, Mom?

Nothing's Wrong

The other night I babysat for my three grandsons while my son and his wife, Anne, went to a costume party. Around midnight I heard the car roll into the garage and they walked into the living room in their '80s rock 'n' roll attire. Since none of us were sleepy yet and Anne had promised me some material for this new-mom book, she told me a story I'd never heard her share before.

Anne's Emotions Run Amok

When I was a tired, overwhelmed new mom, my mother-in-law said the sweetest thing to me. (Mother-in-law? Why, that would be me! I jerked my head up from my note taking. What on earth did I say? She continued as if I wasn't in the room.)

I drove to visit her one day, but I cried the entire way there. And since I'd been bawling all morning and didn't want her—or anyone else—to see my red eyes and tear-stained face, I wore sunglasses and a baseball cap pulled down low.

"What's up, Annie?" she asked when I finally took off my sunglasses. I broke down. "Nothing's wrong. Everything's fine. The baby is fine. Rich is fine. I'm doing fine. But I can't stop crying. I don't know what's wrong with me."

"Aren't hormones just the worst sometimes!" said my mother-in-law.

Such a simple statement—yet immediately I felt heard. Someone understood me and didn't think I was bad. She didn't tell me that I shouldn't feel that way. She didn't tell me what to do differently. She just validated me and my feelings. It was such a relief. I felt so close to her at that moment. I think I threw my arms around her.

I had completely forgotten this. Had Anne not reminded me, I may never have thought of it again. Yet I do agree with the statement I made that day: Being assaulted with not-so-positive emotions caused by fluctuating hormone levels is at best annoying, at times scary, and at worst dangerous.

Physical and Emotional Reality

Have you ever met a new mom who *wants* to have crying jags, angry outbursts, or depressive thoughts? I haven't. I certainly didn't want to feel down after I had my babies, but I did, especially with the first one.

Here's the reality according to medical experts: *Most* new mothers experience the baby blues after delivery. About 1 out of every 10 new moms develops a more severe and longer-lasting depression after giving birth, and 1 in 1,000 women acquires a serious condition called postpartum psychosis.[9]

"There are three types of mood changes women can have after giving birth: The "baby blues," which occur in most women in the days right after childbirth, are considered normal. A new mother has sudden mood

9 http://www.webmd.com/depression/guide/postpartum-depression.

swings, such as feeling very happy and then feeling very sad. She may cry for no reason and can feel impatient, irritable, restless, anxious, lonely, and sad. The baby blues may last only a few hours or as long as one to two weeks after delivery. Postpartum depression (PPD) can happen a few days or even months after childbirth. . . . A woman can have feelings similar to the baby blues—sadness, despair, anxiety, irritability—but she feels them much more strongly. . . . PPD often keeps a woman from doing the things she needs to do every day. When a woman's ability to function is affected, she needs to see her health care provider. Postpartum psychosis is a very serious mental illness that can affect new mothers. . . . Women can lose touch with reality, having auditory hallucinations (hearing things that aren't actually happening, like a person talking) and delusions (strongly believing things that are clearly irrational). . . . Other symptoms include insomnia. . .and strange feelings and behaviors. Women who have postpartum psychosis need treatment right away.[10]

Of course, that's not all that happens when you, your mind, and your body experience childbirth. I remember the nurses at the hospital helping me with my first shower after delivery. I had taken medication during delivery and was still a little groggy when I glanced down at my body. The baby was indeed gone, but I still had a bulging tummy—*and* I was expanding on the top, as well. *Who is this woman?* I recall thinking.

New mother Lucy recently said, "What surprised me the most was that my body started squirting milk everywhere and my belly

10 Ibid.

touched my thighs when I sat down to rock my baby!" Sue developed painful varicose veins, and Janie's hemorrhoids and episiotomy hurt so much that she had to take a pillow with her on every car ride for the next five months. (At least that's the way Janie tells the story!)

Lori's sacroiliac joints malfunctioned, resulting in severe lower back pain. Lynda's abdomen muscle ripped after her fourth baby, and every time she lifted to get out of bed, her upper stomach formed a pyramid. All of these situations were treated eventually. Still, any of these "happenings" is enough to make even the most laid-back mother ask, "Who hijacked my body and emotions?"

Jet-Lagged Moms?

Previously I had a job that necessitated my traveling to the Middle East and Central Asia several times each year. I did everything I could to anticipate and deal effectively with the inevitable jet lag that occurred after those twenty-three-hour-long airplane trips and layovers at the airports. I coped fairly well—usually.

I do remember the time the air conditioning crashed at the terminal where I was stranded for ten hours *after* I had already endured a sleepless cross-the-ocean flight from Egypt. My ankles swelled to triple their normal size, and I developed a rash all over my legs. Not a pretty sight—and one of the unique side effects of jet lag.

Yet the experience that stands out the most is the morning in Cyprus when I had to cancel a prearranged meeting because I just could *not* get out of bed. Talk about jetlag. And I thought I was immune. *Not!*

Dr. Meir Steiner, coauthor of the book *Mood Disorders in Women*, explains a "eureka moment" when he saw the mental connection between the widespread sleep deprivation experienced by many new moms and the postpartum depression that afflicts some of these same women.

In a CBC News release, Dr. Steiner, founder of the Women's Health Concerns Clinic in Hamilton, Ontario, Canada, said, "What these women were describing was jet lag. We called them the jet-lagged moms. The whole system—particularly the hormonal system—is totally desynchronized. . . . The idea is to try and prevent sleep deprivation, which seems to be the biggest enemy for those at risk."[11]

I find it interesting that Dr. Steiner began to suspect a link between sleep deprivation and postpartum depression when pregnant patients shared their fears with him. These mothers who had experienced postpartum depression with their firstborns told him that they were worried about slipping into depression again if they didn't find a way to get more sleep after they brought their new babies home from the hospital.

Oops!

Through the years I've chatted with other moms who've had similar concerns. Mary told me that her postpartum depression is one of the reasons she has only one child. Other mothers have mentioned that their emotional, mental, and physical complications almost deterred them from having more children. And I admit that this all hits a little too close to home for me.

11 " 'Jet-Lagged Moms Prone to Postpartum Depression, Says Doctor," CBS News, accessed Monday, May 25, 2009, http://www.cbc.ca/health/story/2009/05/25/sleep-postpartum-depression.html?ref=rss.

While pregnant with my first child the doctor promised that I'd have a little baby. "Probably about six pounds," he said. "You're a small woman and you've only gained the customary amount." Each time he examined me, he repeated his prediction.

After nearly twenty-four hours of labor, the doctor struggled to get Lynnette out, so he used forceps. When the nurse weighed her, she was 8 pounds 2 ounces. Oops! What happened to that six-pound baby? Guess she grew during labor!

I had a long episiotomy that cut into my rectum, stitches that didn't heal well, and a delayed return to regular elimination. You get the "delicate" picture? One unpleasant memory I have is of me lying on the cold bathroom floor in front of the toilet, writhing in pain.

Anybody out there identify? When I remember the prolonged baby blues I experienced, sleepless nights, isolation, foggy thinking that dogged me during the day, and my inability to ask for what I needed, I guess it's no wonder that I secretly panicked when I contemplated having another baby.

God Is Bigger Than Fear

"Lord, I don't think I can do this again," I prayed. "What if the baby's bigger? What if the labor's long again and they can't get the baby out? What if I'm too tired and sick to take care of Lynnette *and* the new baby? Lord, please help me!"

"Joan, I'll be with you. Trust Me," God seemed to whisper into my heart. I read Deuteronomy 31:8 (NIV), and inserted my name as a reminder that God promised to go before me into the labor and

delivery and that He'd stay and see it through with me. "The LORD himself goes before you [Joan] and will be with you; he will never leave you nor forsake you [Joan]. Do not be afraid; do not be discouraged."

"Okay, Lord. I trust that You'll be with me," I responded in prayer. "Still I'm asking for a smaller baby, a shorter labor, and an easier delivery."

I fully expected God to give me a smaller baby in order to make this all turn out well—like I wanted. And then I had Rich: 9 pounds 4 ounces and 21½ inches long. Now that might not sound big to you. But both times I got pregnant, I weighed under 100 pounds.

A few weeks after Rich arrived, I distinctly remember sitting in church one evening and talking with God. I sensed Him saying, "*See, Joan, I can do it. What you think is too hard, I can achieve. I know you prayed for a small baby. I also know that this baby was bigger. Yet I did what I said I'd do. I never left you. I was right there with you all the time. I helped you. So trust Me. I'm on your side. Now and for always.*"

It's true. God did exactly what He promised. He helped me through the delivery. Instead of twenty-four hours of labor, I had six with Rich. And I recovered much more quickly. No doubt your story is different than mine. Yet God tailored mine for me, to show me that He is bigger than my fear. And He will do the same for you.

> *"Be strong and courageous. Do not be afraid or terrified because of them, for the LORD your God goes with you; he will never leave you nor forsake you."*
>
> DEUTERONOMY 31:6 NIV

Who, Me?

It Is a Big Deal

As new moms—whether you're single or married, a teenager or forty years old—you have this in common: Your mind, body, and emotions are experiencing significant changes. This fact cannot be denied. Whether you adopt or give birth to your child, your life will never quite be the same again.

When you get pregnant, your body makes major modifications to accommodate the growing human being inside you. You gain weight and inches. Joints and ligaments in your pelvic area loosen. Your breasts enlarge, to the delight of some of you and the distress of others. The amount of blood pumped by your heart increases by 30 to 50 percent. Your kidneys work harder. Even your skin pigment darkens. With all these changes, your hormones levels shift—a lot! For example, during pregnancy your progesterone levels maintain an all-time high in order to keep lactation at bay until after delivery.

So if someone (probably a male, but could be anyone!) tries to tell you that it's no big deal and that you merely had a baby and you should get over it and be happy, don't let it get to you. There *is* a lot going on in and around you. You *have* experienced many changes and it *does* take time for it all to settle back to a reasonable facsimile of your prebaby mind and body.

And yes, throughout the centuries many other women have weathered similar changes. You can, too. But remember, you are your own best advocate. Listen to your body, be patient with your spiritual self, pay attention to your emotions, and let it all guide you to make wise personal choices about how to care for yourself. It is the best thing you can do for the baby that you adore.

Making It Personal

Sometimes as a caring new mom, you're so busy taking care of others (baby, older children, husband, ailing parents, or people at work) that you neglect to listen to your body's messages. So take a moment to ask and answer the following questions:

- How does my body feel right now?
- What am I *thinking* about myself, my family, and my circumstances at the moment?
- What emotions am I experiencing? (These can fluctuate, so check it out at different times throughout your week.) Sometimes it's difficult to connect a word to how you're feeling. Perhaps this short list will help you pinpoint your emotions. Are you feeling joyful, anxious, tired, patient, disappointed, nervous, strong, grateful, teary, jumpy, cranky, calm, agitated, alone, confused, annoyed, encouraged, eager, overwhelmed, discounted, loved, relaxed, romantic, stressed?

If you're feeling a little down, that's not unusual for new mothers. Your hormones fluctuate more rapidly after childbirth than at adolescence or at menopause. According to a poll taken by babyzone.com,

39 percent of new moms admit having the baby blues, 22 percent acknowledge they had some of the signs, 34 percent say they didn't get the blues after delivering their babies, and 3 percent aren't sure.[12]

That means over 60 percent know what it's like to have some of the following unpleasant symptoms: sleeplessness, appetite changes, excessive fatigue, decreased libido, frequent mood changes, sadness, loss of pleasure, anger or extreme frustration, withdrawal or isolation, feelings of worthlessness, panic attacks, hopelessness, and helplessness. If these escalate to thoughts of harming yourself or your baby, contact your health professional immediately.

In order to help free yourself from that "hijacked" sensation, ask and answer these additional questions:

- What do I need right now?
- What resources do I have already?
- Who can I share with?

You are important, new mom. Your baby needs you. And your baby loves you no matter what you look like or how you feel. One of the best things you can do for your precious little one is to take care of yourself. Go back to page 99 and read Proverbs 4:23 again. It doesn't matter how other mommies appear to be coping. You have the privilege of monitoring how you're doing and feeling. God loves you and wants you to nurture your baby's mommy.

---

12 "After Your First Child, Did You Get the Baby Blues?" Babyzone Poll (6731 total votes), http://www.babyzone.com/mom_dad/womens_health/depression_post_partum/poll/postpartum-depression-results.

*Don't compare yourself with others.
Each of you must take responsibility for doing
the creative best you can with your own life.*
GALATIANS 6:4–5 MSG

Been There—Done That

Mastitis, Spit-up, and Other Unpleasantries

How do you know when you're a full-fledged member of the New Moms Club? When you hear a baby cry in the grocery store and you start to sway back and forth, back and forth—and then you realize you're merely rocking a loaf of bread because you left your baby home with his dad! Or you accidentally brush your teeth with Desitin. Or you successfully catch spit-up with your hand. Sometimes it's good to laugh about (or at) your reality, even when you're so frustrated with your fluctuating emotions and your changing body issues that you want to scream.

Laughing versus Crying

Shortly after Rich was born, I developed mastitis. If you've not encountered this unpleasantness, here's the scoop. *Mastitis*, inflammation in one or more mammary glands within the breast, usually strikes lactating women. Symptoms include fever, chills, and hot, hard, sore spots in the breast caused by infection or plugged milk ducts. Treatment involves resting, applying warm compresses, and continuing to nurse or express milk frequently. Obviously this helps clear out the milk-plugs. With that background, you'll understand my story better.

When the lumps hardened and the pain deepened, I called my obstetrician. "What should I do?"

"Stop nursing immediately!" he replied. So I obeyed. *(Silly me!)* In a few short hours I had a howling baby and breasts so big and rock-like (clogged with milk) that I had to wrap a couple extra-long beach towels around my chest because (you guessed it) I was leaking like a sieve.

Then *ring-ring-ring.* I picked up the phone. "Hi, Joan! Long time no see," said a voice of a friend from our high school days in Kansas city. "We're in town and thought we'd stop by to say hello and see your new baby."

"Oh, so nice to hear from you. When can you come over?" (Since we now lived in Bakersfield, California, I assumed they'd suggest coming during the upcoming weekend or something like that.)

"We're a block from your house. We'll be there in a few minutes."

Panic! I grabbed a couple fresh towels to replace the used ones so that I didn't reek of dried breast milk. Then I slipped my nicest maternity shirt over my head. You can imagine what a thrill that was, since I'd already packed up anything that reminded me of the twenty-five pounds I'd gained during pregnancy. (Yes, I know that's the normal weight gain! Never mind!)

As soon as I stroked the open lipstick tube across my mouth— that had remained colorless for the last three weeks—the doorbell rang. Richard and I greeted our friends with a smile. They didn't stay long, and after they left I ran into the kitchen so I could blubber alone. Richard followed me. When our eyes met, instead of crying, I burst into laughter. Nodding toward my huge upper body I blurted, "I feel like Dolly Parton!"

At times laughter and lighthearted banter that divert attention from the distress at hand can help more than a trip to the doctor. Seems the wisest man in the world knew that when he wrote, "A merry heart does good, like medicine" (Proverbs 17:22 NKJV).

Yet I readily admit that prescribing laughter to new moms in the midst of deep emotional, mental, or physical pain is not always the best tactic. "Even in laughter the heart may ache, and rejoicing may end in grief" (Proverbs 14:13 NIV).

At the age of twenty, Vanessa became a new mom for the second time:

Certainly sleep deprivation was a bad deal; all those interrupted nights, tired days trying to juggle taking care of my babies, myself, my house, and my husband, all while adjusting to the fluctuating hormones.

But far worse was the abuse and disrespect I experienced. I tried desperately to keep the peace. Sometimes I just gathered the kids in my arms, got into bed, and snuggled with them until the alcoholic rage of their father (my husband) passed. Of course I was depressed.

Crying Has Benefits

Although some of you may never know heart-wrenching pain like this new mom did, if you identify with anything about Vanessa's experience, please know that you don't have to remain in a dangerous situation and endure this kind of treatment. I encourage you to reach out to those who care about you, ask them to help you make a wise plan, and then leave. Your safety and your baby's safety are primary at this point.

The same biblical wise man who proclaimed the benefits of laughter wrote, "Crying is better than laughing. It blotches the face but it scours the heart" (Ecclesiastes 7:3 MSG). So go ahead and cry, if you need to. Find someone who will listen.

Validating a new mom's distress and pain is often the most healing thing a friend or loved one can do. (Remember Anne's story about how her mother-in-law's surprise comment brought her comfort?) Still some people who care deeply about you may not know quite what to do to help you. Asking for what you need is a win-win for you both. You don't have to weather this difficult time on your own, a truth that Melinda discovered after the fact.

Blessed and Baffled Melinda Finds Relief

My long-awaited baby boy started sleeping through the night when he was six weeks old. Everyone told me how blessed I was. I believed them, too. However, my own sleep pattern was goofed up due to hormonal imbalances. I just couldn't seem to sleep. I asked my doctor for help, but he said it would all eventually resolve.

Then one morning when I got out of bed after a fitful night, it felt like someone simply closed all the shades in my house, mind, body, and soul. After that I cried—often. Still I pushed through the darkness on my own for several weeks. I dropped weight that I couldn't afford to lose, so I went to see my obstetrician/gynecologist. He asked a few questions and I started to cry.

"Well, what's wrong with you? Don't you like your baby? Don't you like your husband? Are you mad at him? How do you expect me to help

you?" *Dumbfounded by his reaction to my obvious need, I clammed up.*

"Well, I suppose I could run a blood test, but I don't expect anything to show up. You just need to deal with the changes in your life," he continued. So I went home.

During the next few dark months, I journaled in order to survive. I spent my son's naptimes in prayer. I didn't know it then, but sleeping probably would have been a wiser, God-honoring way to use those afternoons. I had major insomnia and, as it turns out, that is a big indicator of PPD or postpartum depression. I didn't have a label for what I was going through, yet I spent much time and energy trying to get myself out of "it," which unfortunately only made it worse.

After several well-child visits, my son's pediatrician said, "Your baby is thriving. But obviously you aren't. Do you sleep and eat?" I weighed ninety pounds. She said, "I went through something like this. Would you like some medication to help you sort this out?" If I had been breastfeeding my son, I know she never would have suggested I risk his health and try the medication.

Several weeks later (I can be very obstinate!) I decided to take the sleeping pills and for the first time in months, I slept. Every night for almost four weeks. Sleep is good!

One morning when my son was about eight months old, I went to church. There on the back row, I felt the black-out shades lift and I started singing with the others. Energy rushed into my legs, I stood up, and the depression left. I felt like me again.

I still have some residual anger at myself for viewing PPD as a sign of weakness and for not pursuing my options more diligently when I was in the midst of it. Anger that what should have been the happiest time of my life was so much trouble. Anger that someone didn't help me sooner. Ironically, I learned later that many of the people in my life didn't even know anything was wrong!

I wish I would have reached out more. But I didn't. It wasn't easy for me. So I'm working on forgiving myself. I do believe that God made me like I am for a purpose and that He will use my experiences to help other people in similar situations. That gives me hope. Even during my down days, this psalm comforted and reassured me.

> You formed my inward parts; You covered me in my mother's womb. I will praise You, for I am fearfully and wonderfully made; marvelous are Your works, and that my soul knows very well. My frame was not hidden from You, when I was made in secret, and skillfully wrought in the lowest parts of the earth. Your eyes saw my substance, being yet unformed. And in Your book they all were written, the days fashioned for me, when as yet there were none of them. How precious also are Your thoughts to me, O God! How great is the sum of them!
>
> PSALM 139:13–17 NKJV

It's Not Your Fault

Neither the baby blues nor postpartum depression is picky about who it hits. Teenage mothers, older moms, stay-at-home moms, executives, doctors, clergy, or counselors. Christine, a life coach and licensed professional counselor, says:

I had my PPD experience after I had already become a counselor. I think it's strange, but I completely missed the diagnosis of clinical depression. I just thought I was having a hard time adjusting to motherhood even though I had all the PPD symptoms and was not sleeping and had missed days of work.

I assumed most moms had the same difficult time I was having. I guess because it was my first baby, I didn't know what to expect. I did do everything I possibly could to try and kick it. I exercised, ate nutritiously, got out with my baby, went out without the baby. Yet nothing helped. With my psychiatrist's assistance, I realized that I needed medication to get my brain chemistry and hormones back in balance. Within a couple weeks the cloud started to lift. And I was deeply grateful.

Mom, God cares about you—when you're laughing, crying, praising, in a hurry, feeling slow, tired, confused, in pain, joyful, or calm. So when it seems like your body, mind, or emotions have betrayed you, heave your worries about it all over to God. Ask Him to show you what next steps to take. All the resources in the world are at your heavenly Father's disposal, and He wants to share some of these helpful solutions with you.

*Cast all your anxiety on him
because he cares for you.*
1 PETER 5:7 NIV

It's a Juggling Act

Loud and Clear

Our babies let us know when they need or want something. At first they cry in order to communicate with us. Some whimper. Others wail or screech. We listen for their signals to show us when they're hungry, wet, in pain, tired, cranky, or overstimulated. When they feel content, they're usually quiet. This is how it is—at first.

Yet it amazes me how quickly their communications skills develop. Within weeks they smile to express pleasure. Then they coo, follow us with their eyes, reach out their little hands, stick out their tongues, and make faces. It's fascinating. And often comical.

When my oldest grandson was a few months old, I watched him while his parents went out for a few hours. He cried when I put him in his crib, so being the compassionate (or lenient) grandma that I am, I picked him up and held him in the rocker and swayed. He kept losing his pacifier, so I stuck it back in his mouth each time, hoping he'd finally close his eyes and succumb to slumber. *Ha!*

When his eyelids got heavy and he started to doze off, he reached up and grabbed his pacifier and threw it across the room (like a third baseman in training!). I couldn't believe my eyes. I'd never seen him maneuver the pacifier before. I tried to stifle a chuckle, but I couldn't hold it in. I stood up with him in my arms, walked across the room, picked up the binky, rinsed it off (remember I said this was my *first* grandson!), and stuck it in his mouth.

We went back to the rocker and soon he started to doze off again. When he caught himself drifting to sleep, he reached up, snatched the binky from his mouth, and blasted it across the room. I cackled. This kid was communicating to me loud and clear: *I do not want to go to sleep. This binky makes me sleepy, so I'll get rid of it. I just want to stay awake and be with you, Grandma Joan.*

Up-Front

I think it's a funny story (maybe you had to be there). But what's the point? My point is that babies are straightforward when they need or want something. They let us know.

Yet something happens as we grow into adulthood. We start to stifle or code our desires or needs, hoping that the person we're with will read our minds, decode our angry outbursts, tears, or withdrawal, and decipher our dilemma without our having to explain it.

As a new mom, one of the most effective ways you can help yourself (and those you love) is to be up-front about where you hurt, how you feel, and what you need. It's okay to be direct with your doctor, husband, mother, friend, older children, and extended family. Being direct doesn't mean you will whine, demand, pout, yell—or act selfishly.

Although if you do bellyache, sulk, or holler and you feel bad about it, you can take a deep breath, ask for forgiveness if warranted, give it all to God, and move forward to get the help you need. (Maybe it's a nap. Someone to talk to. A massage. A visit to the doctor. A walk. Or take-out food for dinner.)

Practical Tips for Getting Your Body and Emotions Back in Shape

Recently I asked numerous women and healthcare providers for some useful hints about how to cope with the emotional, mental, and physical changes new motherhood brings. Several mentioned the importance of each mommy doing what fits her personality style and family circumstances. What works for your best friend may not work well for you.

On the other hand, there's a benefit in listening to what others find helpful. It may be just what you need and something you never would have thought of. Scan the list of suggested tips. Perhaps something will work out well for you.

1. Move

- Bed exercises: While still in bed at the hospital or birthing center, begin rotating your ankles, feet, and arms. (My own doctor suggested I do a few simple sit-ups before getting out of bed each morning.)

- Walking: To get your body back in shape, start walking around the block as soon as your doctor gives the okay. Leave the baby home with someone. Or push him in the stroller as you walk together as a family.

- Think outside the box: If something like the weather gets in the way of your exercise goal, get creative like this Minnesota mom. When it snowed, they bundled up the baby in a snowsuit, put him in a little plastic baby bathtub, and pulled him as they cross-country skied. Check in with your obstetrician and pediatrician before trying this or other out-of-the-box solutions.

- Exercise class: Sign up for a new-moms exercise class—or a baby and moms class.
- DVD exercise: If it's not convenient to go out to an exercise class, do gentle workouts to an exercise DVD while your baby watches or naps in her car seat or Pack 'n Play.
- Try Christian yoga classes. (Go online for possible classes near you.)
- Aqua exercises: If walking is not your style, try water exercise. It's easier on your joints.
- Seek advice: Ask your exercise-savvy friends about the *movement* tricks that they use. They'd probably love to share their tips with you.
- Relax: Be gentle with yourself. Don't exercise too much too soon. Remember, those celebrity moms who seem to lose baby fat in record time have different lives than most new moms (e.g., personal trainers, chefs, and nannies, not to mention air-brushing experts).
- Make a plan: Staying committed to a wise movement plan can help regulate your hormones and take the edge off the baby blues and mild cases of PPD.

2. Eat

- Consider breastfeeding your baby. (It's good for your child and many studies show that it helps you lose some of the weight you gain during pregnancy.)
- Calorie counting: If you're breastfeeding, experts agree you need at least 1,800 to 2,000 calories a day.

- Eat consistently each day: You don't have to fix gourmet meals. If someone offers to bring you food, gratefully accept. If no one offers, ask your husband to bring home takeout or to grill outside. Make it simple.
- Nutrient-rich foods: To regain your energy and help you feel better, eat nutritious foods like blueberries, salmon, lean beef, low-fat dairy products (yogurt, milk, cheese), brown rice, black beans or kidney beans, oranges, eggs, leafy greens and salads, whole grain cereals.
- Drink lots of water. If water seems blah, squeeze in a lemon, lime, or orange, or add a cucumber or strawberry.

3. Nurture
- Decide: As you love and take care of your baby, make a conscious decision to nurture yourself as well. (Remember Proverbs 4:23.)
- Ask: Share your concerns and needs with your husband and family. Ask for help.
- Vitamins: Continue taking your prenatal vitamins for several more months—or get a high-quality multivitamin to take each day. Consider adding a fish oil capsule to your routine. Ask your pharmacist or nutritionist for advice.
- Speak the truth in love: Remember that the baby blues are quite common. Mental health professionals say that mothers who have the blues need to be allowed to cry if they want to and be permitted to express their fluctuating emotions. It's okay to tell someone that the pull-yourself-together advice

they're giving you is not helpful.

- Embrace hope: Remember that your baby will not stay on this 24–7 schedule forever—and you won't be sleep deprived for the rest of your life.

- Toss stoicism out the window: If the baby blues last longer than a week or two, chat with your health practitioner about your symptoms. You don't have to suffer needlessly. Help is available. And remind yourself that an imbalance in your hormones *doesn't* make you a bad mother.

- Bioidentical hormones: If you sense that your hormones haven't stabilized, consider talking to a hormone specialist. Bioidentical hormones are available through a compounding pharmacy. Although the treatment is controversial, it has helped many women (me included). You might ask at your nearest hospital, women's center, or maternity clinic for the compounding pharmacy nearest you.

- Spiritual changes: Remember that just because you don't *feel* spiritual at the moment (after all, you're exhausted, sleep deprived, and hormonally challenged), you are still the same woman you were before you delivered your baby. God loved you then. He loves you now.

The Lord appeared to us in the past, saying:
"I have loved you with an everlasting love;
I have drawn you with unfailing kindness."

JEREMIAH 31:3 NIV

Safe in God's Arms

God's Gift to Beth

More than anything I wanted to be a mother. When a little girl, I dreamed about it, talked about it. As I grew up, I prayed about it. I knew one day I would hold my baby and smile down into those precious eyes.

And then before I finished college, I became ill. And I didn't get better. We visited many doctors. They gave me numerous tests. Years piled up, one on top of another. One. Two. Three. Four. Five. Six.

"You'll never recover," said the doctor. "And you'll never have children."

My heart broke.

Then after eight years, I started to get better. Gradually I ventured back out into the world beyond my room. I met a fine young man. We dated. Finally in my thirties I got married. I began to hope again that I might realize my dream of being a mother. Maybe.

I talked with my new doctors. "You must get off the medications before you even try to get pregnant," they said. But weaning off the medications wasn't easy. Eventually they gave me the go-ahead. I could get pregnant. It would be safe for both the baby and me. Longing so to be a mother, I felt the anguish each month the test registered negative.

Then it happened. Everything changed. I was expecting. At last I was going to be a mother. My husband and I rejoiced. But I had a terrible nine months. I felt sick every moment of every hour. Still I knew it would be worth it. I'd have a child to love and nurture.

Soon after my fortieth birthday, I experienced the longing of my heart. I was the mother of a beautiful baby girl. My joy knew no bounds. Yet my hormones fluctuated wildly. I had some emotionally rough days when I went home from the hospital.

Then on the ninth day after Micayla was born, I looked in the mirror. One half of my face wouldn't move. Paralyzed. Sudden pain near my ear nearly doubled me over.

We drove to the doctor. He said, "Beth, you have Bell's palsy." I read about it and learned that I had an inflammation of the seventh cranial nerve. Although not all Bell's palsy patients experience pain, I did.

When I tried to smile at my precious baby girl, I couldn't. I looked like I'd had a stroke. I felt like a freak. The pain intensified, and I went back to the doctor. He pressed, pushed, and probed around the area of the paralysis—and I went home with a headache that wouldn't let up.

I went to bed wondering how I could ever take care of my baby. I knew she'd need me to feed, wash, clothe, rock, and love her the next day. It seemed impossible.

That night, I journaled a prayer to God. Lord, don't You remember what I've been through to get to this dream? I'm a mother, and I love that. But now this. I can't even smile at my baby. Maybe she won't want to look at me. How can I care for her? I'm in such pain. Have You forgotten me?

Intense pain kept me from sleeping. Yet I was so exhausted I could hardly move. Then Micayla cried, and I pushed myself out of bed. I picked her up, and she smiled. A genuine smile. Her first. At me. Her lopsided mother. And then I knew: She didn't think I was a freak. In her eyes I was beautiful. She wanted to be with me. I felt her love. She didn't care that I couldn't smile back at her.

My insecurities melted away. Grace filled the room—and my heart. In all the books the experts say that babies smile when they have gas or if they are having a pleasant dream. But this smile was specifically for me. God's gift to me. The turning point I needed.

In the midst of the exhaustion, hormonal fluctuations, depression, and pain, I knew that I was going to be all right—we were going to be all right. That morning I made a vow: I would not *let Bell's palsy steal my joy.*

It took about six months for me to recover from the Bell's palsy. (Even now, four years later, I have some residual drooping.) Yet God heard my prayer. "No, I have not forgotten you, Beth," *He whispered.* "I love you." *He knew I needed tangible evidence of His presence and care, so that morning He gave me an affirming hug through my baby daughter's early smile.*

I want others to know that God loves them deeply. He's a personal God. And to each mother I'd like to say, "God knows what you're going through and He cares. He has not forgotten you."

*Remember your promise to me;
it is my only hope. Your promise revives me;
it comforts me in all my troubles.*
PSALM 119:49–50 NLT

Teach us to number our days, that we may gain a heart of wisdom. . . . Satisfy us in the morning with your unfailing love, that we may sing for joy and be glad all our days. . . . May your deeds be shown to your servants, your splendor to their children. May the favor of the Lord our God rest on us; establish the work of our hands.

PSALM 90:12, 14, 16–17 NIV

Chapter 7

Learning to Tell Time (All Over Again)

What's Up, Mom?

2:00 a.m. Feedings and All

My friend Sandy said:

My husband and I were elated with our baby boy and excited to bring him home from the hospital. Of course, like many new mommies, I felt tired and sore after the labor and delivery. Yet I pushed through my exhaustion to organize his bottles and blankets, change his diapers, and dress him in the little sleeper his grandma and grandpa gave him.

Then I rocked and fed him. He fell asleep in my arms and I laid him carefully in his crib. By that time it was about 8:30 p.m. As I flopped into bed, I reached over to set the alarm for 2:00 a.m. What was I thinking? Or not thinking? I guess I just wanted to be ready. Every time I think about that first night at home with my baby, I laugh. Oh, what I didn't know!

Remember when you spent weeks (okay, months) reading about what to expect and how to care for the new little bundle of joy you soon would bring into your home? You also listened to the advice of friends, relatives, doctors, TV talk show hosts—and even strangers, like the grocery store clerk who fancied herself a baby expert because her sister-in-law just gave birth and invited her into the labor room. Perhaps like Sandy you thought you had it figured out—2:00 a.m. feedings and all.

Then reality set in. That rumored 2:00 a.m. feeding turned into baby-awakenings every two hours or more. Then came holding baby, rocking baby, comforting baby, cleaning baby, listening for baby, changing dirty diapers and bedding, wiping up spit-up, trying to figure out bath time and nursing and formula and naptime and rashes and colic and schedules. You got your days and nights confused, and that's not the half of it. Sometimes you even completely forgot what day it was. Your baby took over the reins of your previously organized (or semi-organized) calendar, and you discovered you had to learn how to tell time all over again.

Runaway Time

I really hate to admit this, because I'm normally not a spacey chick. But here's the deal: As a first-time mommy, I felt a little like I was in kindergarten again, trying to learn how to read the clock and decipher the concept of time. Little hand. Big hand. Digital flashing. Hours. Minutes. *They all ran together.*

I couldn't seem to recall what time I'd last fed my baby, on which breast, when she'd slept or when I'd eaten, or even what time it was at any given moment. For not being a spacey kind of girl, I was acting pretty spacey.

On one spacey afternoon I sat myself down and said, "Joan, you have to pull it together." I took a deep breath, gained a speck of clarity, and asked myself, "Well, what do you need, woman?"

I decided I needed a little notebook that I'd carry around with me so I could record the time of each of my baby's feedings, naps, poopy diapers, *and* my own meal times. But then I got all discombobulated and teary because I didn't have a little notebook and I couldn't figure out when I'd get to the store to buy one. Yeah, I was in sad shape. I think I finally asked my husband to pick one up at the corner drug store on his way home from work.

Time was running away from me, and I wanted it back. I kept my little black spiral notebook in my pocket or on the table beside the rocker. I tried to write down what time the clock "said" each time I nursed. But then I got even more confused because I didn't know whether to count the time of the feeding from when I started nursing, like perhaps 11:55 p.m., or when I finished at 12:40 a.m. And since the how-to manuals admonished me to switch breasts each feeding in order to maintain sufficient milk supply on both sides, I felt it mandatory to write that down as well. But I couldn't remember which breast I last nursed Baby on.

It had all seemed so simple when I merely *read* about being a mom. Actually *being* a mom was a little more complicated. And time wasn't cooperating—in any way, shape, or form.

Like my friend Jenne said, "It didn't matter how hard I tried, I was always late. I had never in my life had a problem with time—or being late—until my baby arrived. Not only was my timetable all messed up, but the baby always seemed to have issues at the most inopportune times!"

Good News/Bad News

After the baby came, I felt that I really needed more time in my day and then I realized that I had all the time I was ever going to get.

Bummer. In retrospect, I can identify with one of my Facebook friends who recently posted, "Okay, I need twenty-nine hours in my day. Is that asking too much? Just five more hours. Please, pretty please."

This thought has probably flashed through the minds of many new moms who feel behind and need more time to sleep, play with baby, connect with their guy, sleep, cook, clean, plan, sleep, check in with friends, and finish their work before the boss has a fit. *You know what I mean?*

It's a good news/bad news issue. First the disappointing news: If you're hoping to grab an extra hour or more, it's not going to happen. God won't change His universal plan to give you more hours in each day.

I knew this down deep, but when I read a quote from the wisest man who ever lived, I began to stop my tug-of-war with time. "God has already planned what now exists. He has already decided what man is. A man [or woman] can't argue with the One who is stronger than he [she] is" (Ecclesiastes 6:10 NIrv).

The good news? God, the Stronger One, designed that you and I live within the boundaries of time and space to protect us from overload and burnout. We actually need these parameters to help us live in harmony with our humanness. It's like God is saying, "_____ (fill in the blank with your name), I love you and I care when you're feeling overwhelmed. You don't have to do it all or know it all and take care of it all. You don't have the time, energy, and wisdom for it all. So relax, do what you can, when you can, with the limited stamina you have for any current task or interaction. I'm big enough to handle the rest."

*But I trust in you, L*ORD*;*
I say, "You are my God."
My times are in your hands....
Let your face shine on your servant;
save me in your unfailing love.

PSALM **31:14–16** NIV

Who, Me?

Living in the Baby Time Zone

Regardless of how much prebaby planning you did to assure that your child would not alter your lifestyle and schedule, the truth is: Baby changes things. If you're a new mom it doesn't matter whether the state where you live is in the Eastern, Central, Mountain, or Pacific Time Zone (or somewhere else in the world) because you move, eat, and sleep (or try to) in the Baby Time Zone.

Baby has 24–7 needs. And you, Mommy (although you may have great help), are the one in charge. There may be exceptions to this, but since you're reading this new-mom book, the buck probably stops with you whenever your baby is concerned. Calendars, schedules, agendas, daily goals, and even simple to-do lists seem to go haywire when Baby moves in. At first you might be able to play it by ear, but within a few weeks, many moms find it stressful to never feel in control of their time schedules.

Yet each woman approaches her time and her mommy role a little differently. Understanding your preferences helps you choose what kind of time-management ideas fit you—and releases you from feeling the pressure to structure yourself and your baby in the same way your best friend, sister, mom, or mentor might do it. Although there are more scientific assessment tools available to help you understand your temperament and behavior styles, you can save that kind of discovery for later. *'Cuz you probably just don't have the time right now!*

Make It Personal

For a brief overview of how you approach managing your life and time, answer these simple questions. Circle (on the page or in your mind) the questions or statements that best describe you. Read each of the couplet questions below and think about which most represents what you *prefer* to do. (Or if you're feeling just too tired and spacey right now skip this section and go straight to the "Been There—Done That" section. It's okay! *Really*.)

A.
1. Are you recharged by activity, interaction, and conversation with others? OR
2. Do you gain renewed energy by being and working alone or one-on-one and by writing down your thoughts?

B.
1. Do you like to make immediate decisions and have a motto something like "Let's get going. We've got lots to do"? Do you feel stressed when you're forced to slow down and do nothing for extended periods of time? OR
2. Are you more comfortable discovering all the possibilities and reflecting before you decide and have a motto similar to "If something's worth doing, it's worth taking time and doing it well." Do you get physically and emotionally drained when you feel pushed into including too many fast-paced activities on your calendar for too long?

C.

1. Would you rather focus on the facts and figures about a problem/issue and like to organize your agenda and stick to the plan? OR

2. Do you notice your feelings easily, like to tell stories, and focus on what others are doing and feeling before you try to figure out solutions?

Give Yourself a Break

After reflecting on your answers to the above questions, what would you say about your mommy-self right now? Remember, whatever you surmise at the current time is not set in stone. You're an adaptable woman, and you just might think and react differently at another season of your life. Give yourself a break.

Remember when I sat myself down and asked, *"Well, Joan, what do you need right now?"* My spontaneous response was "a little spiral notebook." Pretty simple, huh? Now it's your turn. When it comes to your current baby time-schedule-related issues, what do you need? What's the first thing that pops into your brain? *Nothing?* Well then, what's the second thing that pops into your mind?

There are no right or wrong responses to these questions, so relax. New moms can move away from the it's-either-black-or-white thinking. When it comes to scheduling and timing in your motherhood role, do what works for you and your family.

Annette offers this relaxed counsel after being a "new mom" four different times.

Annette's Advice

I try not to be overly concerned about what others think about my mothering and baby scheduling decisions.

For example, with my first baby I tried to execute all the advice in the how-to manuals. Frequently I read, "You should sleep every time your baby sleeps." I literally raced to bed whenever my baby daughter closed her eyes. My rigid insistence on heeding this recommendation left absolutely no time for my husband and me to chat or be together. Eventually I discovered a happy-medium naptime schedule that worked for me. I slept during each afternoon nap and stayed up to enjoy some couple time when she fell asleep in the early evening.

I learned new flexible solutions with each baby. Since I knew that my fourth child would be my last, I wanted to savor each moment with her. Consequently, I made a decision that others didn't agree with. For the first year of her life I made a plan to sit near the back of the church sanctuary each Sunday and hold my baby during the services. If she cried, I left. I didn't take her to the nursery until she turned one year old. It worked for me, but I realize it might not be a scheduling/timing decision other moms would make. I suggest each mom do what is least stressful for her.

Each time I'm faced with another timing and scheduling dilemma— and there's always another—I remind myself that It's just a phase. This, too, shall pass. Then my shoulders relax a little, and I start to breathe more deeply.

Juggling Takes Practice

New mom, listen to your own needs, desires, and advice. You're your own best advocate. And you're smarter than you think you are. You know and care more about your baby, family, and yourself than anyone else does. Ask for help and suggestions from others you respect. Go ahead and try the ideas that seem to fit your daily situation. If any idea works, great. If the advice doesn't fit you, it's okay to toss it aside. You can try it again later—or not.

Finally, trust God to give you the wisdom, discernment, and guidance that you want and need at this current season of your life. No matter how you handle your new mommyhood, it *is* a juggling act. And the skill of juggling doesn't come automatically: It takes practice. Please cut yourself some slack.

Been There—Done That

Darcy's Challenge

To steal a line from Oprah, "one thing I know for sure" is that parenthood is a lesson in learning one's limits. Before my baby arrived, there were very few things I couldn't handle on my own. I had life, time, and schedules under control. Then came motherhood! Suddenly I noticed my weaknesses and vulnerabilities.

I've been back to work full-time for two weeks now. It's as challenging as I heard it would be. I can't be in two places at once. I'm either home, en route, or at work. I feel torn. I really enjoy being engaged with work again, and yet I miss Abby. She does something new every day, and I'm not the one to see her to do it.

Yesterday after advising—well, more like bossing—our day-care provider, who happens to be Abby's daddy and my husband, about her eating and naptime schedule, he reminded me that I'm not here from 8:00 a.m. to 6:00 p.m. "You can't control what you don't see, hear, and touch. There are just some things that will be a little different when I'm home with her during the day," he said. "Please trust me."

It's difficult. After all, I had her inside me for nine months and right beside me for thirteen weeks while on maternity leave. I'm still trying to figure out this work/home balance thing.

Although Darcy chose to balance her time between full-time work and being at home with her baby, Jodi chose a slightly different route. According to Jodi, "no" isn't forever.

I keep reminding myself that by saying yes to one thing, I need to say no to something else. I can't do it all. So I've just said no to a promotion in order to keep my work at a part-time level where I can say yes to spending larger chunks of the day with my third baby. I want to be confident in my no and to be committed to my yes. Here's what helps me. My no isn't a forever decision: It's just for now. I keep telling myself this.

Darcy's and Jodi's experiences show that learning how to tell time all over again and to make plans and agendas as a new mom means making adjustments. It sounds simple, but it can include some minor and major modifications. Betsy was accustomed to scheduling and attending continual meetings and work appointments before her baby came. "I keep fighting my conditioned feeling that I should be somewhere at a certain time, but I really have nowhere to be!" she shared. "Such a weird feeling for me!"

Time Management Ironies
New mom Leslie told me how disappointed she was when she missed her favorite monthly moms' support group the other night, just because "I lost track of what day it was. My eleven-week-old cries a lot with tummy aches and allergies. My nights and days mix together right now."

Allie said, "I'm just amazed at how much longer it takes me to get out the door to go anywhere with my little guy. So I've decided to change one of my time-management planning questions from 'When do I need to leave?' to 'When do I need to be backing out of the driveway?' "

"When our third child was born," said Lori, "someone gave me a book about time management for parents. The advice worked beautifully, so I assumed I finally had the parenting of babies all figured out. *Not.* Our fourth child came along fifteen months later and I realized I knew practically nothing about parenting. Each child is so different. The schedule that works for one doesn't necessarily work for the next one. It's like starting all over again."

Another new mom named Macie e-mailed me to share, "I've always been quite organized in scheduling my tasks. I had cooking, cleaning, and laundry planned for specific times on specific days. But what surprised me and threw me off the most was how much laundry a little person makes! Obviously there were other things about mommyhood that proved tricky, but seriously—scheduling and doing laundry was a biggie for me!"

Bess said, "You gotta schedule, schedule, schedule. As soon as my babies were a couple weeks old, I put each one on a schedule. Literally it was one of my survival skills. As they grew up, they knew what to expect, and I knew how to schedule my work, meetings, and phone calls."

Cynthia agreed. "Get a plan. Write things out. Make lists. Make sure your spouse reads it so you're on the same page. Streamline everything!"

Laissez-Faire or Structured Mamahood

Yet normally-laid-back Allison felt stressed when she tried to squeeze herself and her baby into a four-hour feeding schedule. When she backed off and fed her little one when he was hungry instead of when the so-called experts insisted she must, everyone relaxed and enjoyed life more.

Janene had personality tendencies similar to Allison. Instead of relishing making lists and schedules and heeding minute details, she felt more comfortable looking for the art or story in her days. It didn't matter to her if her baby had on a new outfit when visitors came or if the clothes were folded just right. Although she knew the value of keeping things clean, she stayed content with what her meticulous sister called "laissez-faire mamahood."

Whether you're naturally people-oriented or task-oriented, fast-paced or slow-paced, talkative or reflective, structured or spontaneous, as a new mom you may have been a little flabbergasted by how many adjustments you needed to make and how befuddled you felt about trying to fit it all in and figure it all out, at least at first.

At the beginning of chapter 3, I told the story of how breast-feeding came fairly easy to me, even though I hadn't planned to do it. I also mentioned that some women don't find it that simple and I'd share about that later. Now's the time.

Say What?

Unlike me, Lynne decided long before she delivered her son that she wanted to nurse him. She talked about it. Read about it. Dreamed about it. Yet in the hospital when the nurses tried to help Lynne, baby Donnie wouldn't latch on. Not the first time or the twentieth. Lynne felt disappointed but determined. They tried repeatedly, and finally she had to leave the hospital without successfully nursing her baby.

At home she tried each day. Nothing worked. Her husband helped by tickling Donnie's feet, encouraging Lynne, bringing her drinks and food, and making phone calls to ask what to do. Days dragged on while Lynne faithfully pumped to keep up her milk supply. Daddy fed Donnie from a bottle, but the baby lost weight. Lynne sank deep into depression. She tired of trying, lost sleep, and wondered where she had gone wrong. Two months later, still determined to fulfill her dream of breastfeeding her son, Lynne called the La Leche League again.

The helpful lady on the phone said, "Put your baby on your breast."

"I did. I have. I am. It isn't working," said Lynne, crying into the receiver.

"We'll send someone out to your house to help," said the woman. "What is your address?"

"It's 5555 North Elm Street in Blossom City." Lynne gave her the address of the home where they had lived for two years.

"Okay, would you give me the cross streets and directions, please?"

"Uhhhh. Well, you take. . .ummm. Well, I can't remember. Let me think. You turn on. . .ummmm." Tears rolled down Lynne's cheeks as her mom and sister stood nearby and tried to help. Lynne panicked. "Oh I don't know. I don't know where I live. I don't know what day it is. I don't know what time it is. I barely know my own name."

Lynne and her family chuckle about it now, but it really didn't seem humorous at the time. "Here I was a normally competent, energetic teacher who successfully managed twenty-five active second graders, wrote daily time plans, scheduled curriculum for months in advance, and I literally didn't know which day of the week it was. I was just so tired.

"The good news is that we finally figured out how to help Donnie nurse. He did gain weight and even flourished during the next few months of nursing. Eventually I got some rest, things normalized, and I discovered how to tell time again."

God saw Lynne and her husband when they were having so much trouble trying to figure out how to nourish Donnie. He saw their determination, disappointment, confusion, and exhaustion. Sometimes it's hard to understand why God doesn't intercede sooner. Yet you and I live in an imperfect world where everything doesn't always work out exactly as we dreamed, planned, or timed it would.

God cares about every detail of your life. He cares about your time schedule, your calendar, your plans, your uncertainty, and your exhaustion. You matter more to Him than all the other beautiful areas of His awesome creation.

*"Look at the birds, free and unfettered,
not tied down to a job description,
careless in the care of God. And you count
far more to him than birds."*
MATTHEW 6:26 MSG

It's a Juggling Act

Time: Friend or Foe?

All new moms encounter a similar predicament: too much to do and learn and not enough time to figure it all out and do it. *Time management* is how we resolve this dilemma. Each day (it may seem like each second) in your new role as mommy, you're faced with choices about what to do and what not to do.

Several years ago I became fascinated with the idea of developing a friendship with time instead of continuing to view time as an enemy. I noticed that my tendency to over expect, overdo, over try, and overcommit were based on misconceptions I had about the reality of time. I think I sometimes tried to live outside the boundaries of time—thinking and believing that I *should* be able to do everything or anything that someone asked or suggested I do. Of course, I really wanted to do it all "just right" for the good of my family and God.

However, I started to see how impossible that was. I couldn't just read another how-to manual and get more organized in order to stuff more good work into a restricted amount of time. Neither could I succeed in adding more hours to my day.

Time Management or Self-Management

You and I cannot control time. You cannot control when your baby cries, needs you, wakes up, or gets sick. However, you can control and be responsible for yourself, your responses, your well-being, and your actions. You have that privilege. So, although you cannot manage time, you *can* manage, supervise, take care of, direct, and regulate your self—your own decisions, choices, beliefs, behaviors, habits.

Time management is actually self-management. It's a liberating reality—and doable. You have the privilege of making choices about how you care for yourself and your baby. Below are a few suggestions from other new moms. Skim them. Feel free to implement what sounds like it might work for you.

Remember, you do have options. To each idea, you can say yes or no or you can renegotiate how to do it, or you can respond with "I don't know. Let me think about it."

Random Time (or Self-) Management Tips

1. Adjust expectations.

- About planning and communication: Share and discuss plans, tasks, and ideas with your spouse so you'll both be on the same page, especially for the things that pertain to your family.
- About to-do lists: One young couple decided to try to accomplish just one task per day other than the normal baby care and self-care.
- About cooking: Instead of expecting to eat three-course meals like in your before-baby times, try eating something simple like egg sandwiches or ham and cheese wraps for dinner—at least in the first few weeks or months of your baby's life.
- About positive self-talk and reinforcement: At first even

taking a shower or washing your hair is an achievement.

Set realistic, small goals for your day and then congratulate yourself when you accomplish them. (Even if you would have done the task twelve times faster in your pre-mommy days.)

- About saying no: Postpone saying yes to big projects that you'd enjoy doing later but wouldn't be wise to tackle right now. One new mom said no to being the director of vacation Bible school until the next year. Another delayed putting her house on the market and moving until her baby was eight months old. Even then she knew it would be a major commitment.

- About gifts and thank-you notes: One young mother asked for a reprieve in sending handwritten thank-you notes when she opened the gift in front of the giver.

2. Accept help.

- When others offer to help, say yes.
- Keep a simple to-do list handy so that after saying yes to someone's offer of help, you can hand him or her the list. Be specific about what to suggest the helpers do—fold laundry, load and empty the dishwasher, refill the diaper bag, drop library books in the return slot, take your older child to the park, take the baby for a walk in the stroller while you catch a thirty-minute nap.

3. Buy yourself some moments of relief.

- Try bathing or showering with your baby. Saves time and turns the often stress-filled-kitchen-sink-baby-bathing experience into a time of parent-infant bonding. Works for either mommy or daddy.

- Chunk-a-cize the time-consuming tasks. Break larger projects into fifteen- to thirty-minute increments. For example: Set a timer for ten minutes to clear off one counter where you've thrown your mail. When the timer dings, you're done. Then you can come back to it later, if you need to.

- One new mommy said the tip that helped her the most was using drive-through and curbside services whenever she could at the pharmacy, bank, or restaurant.

- Order groceries and other necessities online. Many offer free delivery services.

- Although you will want to be wary of overdoing any multitasking, you might wish to try these simple ideas: Read or write a letter while waiting for an appointment or in line to pick up older children from school or activities. Straighten your desk while on the phone with a friend. Pray while on a walk—even aloud while pushing the stroller. Read a devotional book while nursing. Rock and sing to your toddler while nursing your baby.

Safe in God's Arms

Baby Jesus Grows Up

Jesus arrived as a cuddly and dependent infant, just like your child. His mother, Mary, and adoptive father, Joseph, nurtured, fed, rocked, bathed, and clothed him. No doubt He woke them up in the wee hours of the night and cried at inconvenient times, just as your baby does. Perhaps Mary got tired and a little confused about how best to schedule His naptimes and guide Him, too. After all, He was her first baby. She was young and inexperienced, even though she may have helped babysit other children during her teenage years.

We don't know much about Jesus' toddler and childhood days, but what we do know (from Dr. Luke's account of Jesus' life) is that Jesus grew relationally, physically, and spiritually. He also developed discernment, character, and understanding in how to handle life's multifaceted circumstances. "And Jesus grew in wisdom and stature, and in favor with God and man" (Luke 2:52 NIV).

Developing Balance

By His Son's example, God confirms that He cares about every area of your days, not just the spiritual parts. New mom, He wants to help you find *balance* in this joyous yet perplexing time of your life. Still, the God who created all things knows that balance itself has no specific objective. It's a constant state of motion and flex. To help you understand this, imagine the following:

- You stand up and spin around three times.
- You jog in place for a minute and hop to the corner of the room and back.
- You whirl around twice more.
- Then immediately you endeavor to balance on one foot.

Now visualize the subtle adjustments you have to make in your foot and body to maintain equilibrium. This imaginary exercise can help you picture what you're attempting to do in balancing the different aspects and roles of your life during any given day with your baby, family, life, and work. Developing balance with the constant give-and-take is a skill.

Consider asking God to help you cultivate this time (self-) management skill. You can do it. You are safe in His arms. Remember God cares about every hour of your life—and not just the church and prayer part. In fact, every moment of your day is worthy of prayer and God-partnership.

Take your everyday, ordinary life—your sleeping, eating, going-to-work, and walking-around life—and place it before God as an offering. Embracing what God does for you is the best thing you can do for him. Don't become so well-adjusted to your culture that you fit into it without even thinking. Instead, fix your attention on God. You'll be changed from the inside out.

ROMANS 12:1–2 MSG

God is love. When we take up permanent residence
in a life of love, we live in God and God lives in us.
This way, love has the run of the house,
becomes at home and mature in us. . . .
There is no room in love for fear.
Well-formed love banishes fear. . . .
First we were loved, now we love.

1 JOHN 4:17–19 MSG

Chapter 8

Redefining Love— Reducing Stress

What's Up, Mom?

Love Doesn't Fit in a Box

What is love—really? I mean there's friendship love, marriage love, sentimental love, tough love, a father's love, healthy self-love, love for God, love for the unlovely, mother's love, Jesus' model of love, Hollywood-type love, and if-you-really-valued-and-honored-me-you'd-do-what-I-say love (sometimes used by husbands and wives, friends, pastors, and parents when they want something from us, but that's another book).

I realize that God's character is love's bottom line. And I've read and studied the 1 Corinthians 13 definition of love as many times as I've heard it recited in sermons and at baby dedications and weddings (mine included). Still it seems that any attempt to put explanations of love on paper only bounce off the page and walk confidently away. *Love* won't be confined. Yet we try to limit it.

So the other day when I posted the following questions on my Facebook page, it's because I am genuinely interested in people's take on love. I asked: "How would you describe the love you have for your children? And how did having kids redefine love for you?"

I received several sincere responses, including a private message from Juliet, the working mom of two little ones. (There's that oxymoronic phrase again: *working mom*. You and I both know that all conscientious mothers *work*. It's just that my friend Juliet works at a full-time job outside her home as well as being a full-time mommy for her little son and daughter).

Juliet's Out-of-the-Comfort-Zone Love

I think the words that Juliet wraps around her story come close to explaining the mysterious nature of a mother's love and how it redefines her life and devotion. Here's the essence of what Juliet wrote:

One night several years ago, sitting alone in my apartment, I cried to God, "Lord, I have so much capacity to love and no one to give it to. I'm grateful for my family and good friends, yet they don't absorb that cavernous space inside me that longs to love a husband and my own children. I'm afraid. What if I never have kids?"

I sensed God's whisper in my spirit: "Juliet, it's all right. I'll give you the kids that I have in mind for you." *My shoulders relaxed as peace swept into my soul. I held on to that assurance for a couple more years until I started dating the man I finally married. To my surprise, I experienced a depth of emotion I'd never imagined. Out of nowhere sometimes I cried when we got together. I had assumed genuine romantic love would be warm and fuzzy. Instead I sometimes felt overwhelmed and confused. It's like my heart woke up, and these unfamiliar feelings emerged.*

Then we had kids and love stunned me again—with even more force. Our adopted daughter resisted sleep, perhaps because of her shaky entrance into the world. I wanted to reassure her, so I rocked her for an hour or more at each nap and bedtime. Sometimes we both cried as I tried to figure out the weird reality of my newfound love. Again I thought that love would feel cozy, comfortable, and happy, but my mother-love proved complex and laced with doubt about whether I could do it.

Soon after that I got pregnant with our son and because I went into preterm labor, the doctor put me on bed rest. During those three months in bed, I prayed, "God, please. I beg You, spare my child's life."

And it happened again. "Juliet," *God whispered,* "I haven't changed My mind. I still promise that I'll give you the children I have in mind for you." *Lucas arrived healthy when I delivered him at thirty-nine weeks. God kept His promise, of course. He gave me two wonderful babies, first through adoption and then through an extremely difficult pregnancy.*

Just yesterday I sat on the couch, petting the asthmatic dog that we almost lost several times. And I remembered my cry to God when I was single about how I desperately wanted children and a family. I now have so much to love—my husband, my sweet kids, and even my silly dogs.

My ideas of love have completely changed. I now know that love can be hard, perplexing, and sometimes just plain painful. It's not syrupy or fuzzy-warm. At times love doesn't feel so good—when I'm sleep-deprived, overwhelmed, and exhausted.

Love pushes you out of your comfort zone to a place where you feel indecisive and unprepared. However, love also stretches and grows you beyond who you could have been if the world had stayed centered around you.

I'm still sorting out the realities of what this all means for me. As difficult as these few years have been, I wouldn't trade my kids for anything, especially not an easier life.

Change Happens

Perhaps like Juliet, your ideas of life and love have shifted from that once delightful yet distant vision of having children to the meaningful but noisy reality you face each day as a new mom. Throughout this book, we've explored how becoming a mommy alters you—your life and work, your relationships, your spirituality, your emotions, and your body. In addition, being a mommy modifies the way you make decisions, how you spend your time, how you relate to your husband, how you sleep—or don't sleep.

You're learning to love at a deeper (and perhaps more uncomfortable) level. You've become devoted to your baby and his or her well-being. And you've discovered that all this love-induced commitment is loaded with change. Well, not just change, but *change*!

Turning Point

As a new mom, you're experiencing one of life's major turning points. So what's the big deal about a turning point? Remember? TPs turn your life in a direction, for better or worse, toward or away from something where the future is not going to be a continuation of the past. Every turning point—including motherhood—has spiritual, emotional, mental, relational, educational, and physical implications.

Stress Happens

And the practical reality of CHANGE is that it brings stress. (Okay, not just *stress*, but STRESS.) Stop for just a moment. Take a deep breath. If you're feeling a little—or a lot of—stress, give yourself a mental break. When you're a new mom, stress happens! You're not a bad mom because you feel stressed out sometimes.

Perhaps you've been conditioned to think of stress as purely negative. Yet any genuine discussion of stress will mention *eustress* (good stress) as well. For example, getting a raise and promotion at work (which can render eustress) can be equally as stressful as losing in the quest for the new position or agreeing to take a pay cut or even getting laid off (distress).

Juliet felt distress when she contemplated never getting married or having children. She also experienced stress (both distress and eustress) with the mixture of experiences around the adoption of her baby girl and the complication in her pregnancy and second baby.

Stress Defined

So what's your definition of change-induced stress? The American Institute of Stress maintains that the most popular definition of *stress* is "a condition or feeling experienced when a person perceives that demands exceed the personal and social resources the individual is able to mobilize."[13]

What? Where have I been all my life? I think I just moved from my lifelong guilt-producing misbelief that "Joan, you shouldn't be feeling stressed" to "Oh my, Joan, stress is merely you reaching the limits of your humanness and imperfection." I can feel my shoulders relax again.

---

13 "Stress, Definition of Stress, Stressor, What is Stress?, Eustress?" AIS (The American Institute of Stress), http://www.stress.org/topic-definition-stress.htm?AIS=1252a3842a5d9545e08df491f128240c.

Your Ultimate Resource

This all just proves again that I'm not God. I can't live optimally without adequate sleep, nutrition, and respite. I can't foresee all things. Or handle all problems perfectly all the time. That would be God's MO.

This mothering role can push you and me to our limit, no doubt about it. With all the inherent changes, losses, and learning curves that are a natural part of motherhood, we feel the stress. Any caring, conscientious human mother would.

Yet I have a resource that is bigger than me. And you have a resource that is bigger than you, too. Bigger than your confusion, greater than your strength, and deeper than your love. *God.* He's your Ultimate Resource. When everything becomes unmanageable, turn it over to Him. His love never changes. He went to great lengths to show you His Love when He sent His Son.

No matter what you're experiencing with your new baby or family, God's renewing power reaches you. Give Him your life. Your baby. Your stress. Your fears. Your hope.

Can anything ever separate us from Christ's love?...I am convinced that nothing can ever separate us from God's love. Neither death nor life, neither angels nor demons, neither our fears for today nor our worries about tomorrow—not even the powers of hell can separate us from God's love. No power in the sky above or in the earth below—indeed, nothing in all creation will ever be able to separate us from the love of God that is revealed in Christ Jesus our Lord.

ROMANS 8:35, 38–39 NLT

Who, Me?

Shocked

In chatting with moms, I've noticed a common viewpoint that sounds something like this: "I'm a mom—and it's a beautiful, God-given thing. So if I love, give, trust, and work like I should, then everything will be fine, the baby will be calm, our family will work together, and we'll all be happy." And when this doesn't happen just as mom imagined it would, then shock, disappointment, and guilt come calling. *Ugh!*

This often leads to self-talk like, *I can't do this. What's wrong with me? I should be able to handle this. My husband's disappointed in me. What am I doing? Is God mad at me?*

Anita's Love Ride

I talked with God about having children. My husband and I discussed it. I always dreamed of being a mother. So I plunged in, got pregnant, and had little Matthew. My world became a blur. I do recall thinking, What have I done? I'm supposed to love this baby. I don't feel it. Why's he crying all the time? I'm too tired. I'm too young. What am I going to do?

I saw other mothers doing it all—gushing about their babies and how much they adored them and loved being a mother. Somehow I thought I should be able to go on with my life the same as before. But I did everything wrong—or so I thought. I didn't want anyone to see how confused and unloving I felt.

When my sister came to town with her twelve-month-old, I suggested we have our babies' portraits professionally taken. Matthew was just two weeks old. Ever since we'd brought him home from the hospital, he had cried. Just trying to get him (and myself) ready for the photo shoot upset me. He wouldn't stop screeching. I felt like throwing him out the window. Of course I'd never do that.

Then my sister called and said, "Just wanted to let you know that Ashley has a runny nose this morning."

"Okay," I responded and hung up the phone.

Then I totally freaked out. A runny nose? What's that mean? Now what? Will he get sick? What do mothers do? I can't let my baby cry in public. I'm such a bad mother. Blah-blah. Cry-cry. Sniff-sniff.

I managed to get us loaded into the car, then drove to the studio and got the cousins' picture taken. Surprisingly, Mathew stopped crying for the shoot!

After another three weeks with minimal sleep and near-constant wailing (from both of us!), we discovered Matthew had colic. We made some revisions to my diet (I was breastfeeding), and we both got some rest.

Then it happened. Matthew smiled. Not just any smile at anybody. He smiled at me. He sees me. He likes me. He feels safe with me. He's okay. I'm not a terrible mom.

He smiled, and I fell in love. And although it was not all smooth sailing from that moment on, I settled down a bit and started to enjoy my love-ride with my baby son.

Making It Personal

For some moms the love rushes in right after they give birth. Yet for others, like Anita, the feelings of love lag behind. No matter what your circumstances, becoming a new mother means change, and with that comes occasions of stress. That is completely normal. (Oh how I wish someone would have told me that during my harried months and years as a new mom!)

Becoming aware of your unique situation helps. It can lead you to make choices to diffuse the inevitable side effects of stress. Skim this partial list of possible causes of new-mom stress and circle (or make a mental note of) the ones that you experience.

1. **Time demands:** Round-the-clock tending to your baby's needs, while attempting to take of yourself, your husband, your family, the house, and all your other obligations. It's often impossible to fit it all into a twenty-four-hour day.

2. **Finances/money/overdue bills:** Pregnancy, doctors, hospitals, equipment, supplies all cost money. Budget adjustment due to decreased income if mom takes a leave of absence or goes part-time or quits her job to stay home with baby. Worries about credit card debt and loans. Rising cost of living.

3. **Relationship demands:** Older children to take care of. Blended families to navigate. Friends who feel bad because you don't have time for them. Aging parents who need your

help. Husbands who feel left out, don't understand your stress, and demand things be done. In some cases, family members' addiction, abuse, and health problems.

4. **Illness/postpartum issues/C-section recovery:** Baby blues, depression, delivery or surgery complications, sleep deprivation, breastfeeding issues, and related illnesses. Plus possible health-related problems of infants and older children.

5. **Work/school:** A job outside the home and/or you or your spouse attending school. Potential feeling of isolation and changing identity issues if you have resigned from your job. Wondering what others think about your decisions regarding work/school.

6. **Life:** Self-doubt, worries about the economy, declining culture, and what it will mean for your child's future. Normally enjoyable things like taking part in your hobbies, passions, interests, and church, volunteer service, Bible study, or quiet times you no longer have energy or time for.

7. **Tragedy:** Facing death or the life-threatening illness of a loved one, marriage problems, divorce, job loss, moving, leaving friends.

So, new mom, please be gentle with yourself. As you contemplate each of the areas that you circled, ask yourself, "What support resources (people, places, or things) do I have to help me cope in this specific stress area?" For example:

- Nanette had a sister and mother living nearby whom she asked to do specific chores. This alleviated her stress related to new time demands.
- Bethany realized that God had placed her husband in her life to support and protect her, and she decided to be more consistently upfront about sharing her fears and asking for his help.
- Although Christina had just recently moved to a new town and didn't know many people, she went to the moms group at the church down the street and found new friends to support her during her premature baby's illnesses.
- Tina acknowledged that music had been her friend and comfort before she had children, so she made sure she listened to her favorite singer when she felt overwhelmed.
- Kristen found a doctor who specializes in treating her type of headaches and found some relief.
- Karla asked for references from her friends and church members and then went to see a Christian counselor to help her deal with the grief she experienced after her mom died.

What would help you at this time in your life? Ask God for clarity and take an intentional step in that direction.

Been There—Done that

Love Redefined

How did having kids redefine love for you? Remember when I posted this question on my Facebook page? Jodi responded, "I felt a new love for my own mother within hours of having my firstborn and felt a need to apologize to her for not fully appreciating the love that she showed me as a child."

Mary Lou wrote, "I never understood God's *agape* (unconditional) love until I held my own baby in my arms."

"I felt hugged by God after I held and loved my own babies. Now through the ups and downs of the following years, I've repeatedly sensed God's hug," responded Terry.

Betsy wrote, "I heard someone say that having children is like having your heart walking around outside your body! That's true for me. I feel more vulnerable—like my life is more fragile, my purpose deeper, my time more precious. And with all this, my faith and reliance on my Savior becomes even more critical."

Mommy/Grandma/Baby

Perhaps Timothy's mother, Eunice, would agree with Betsy. We don't know much about Eunice and her situation, yet we do know that Timothy arrived during a volatile time for Christians. It must have been stressful for believers in Jesus like Eunice to practice their faith.

New-mom Eunice's husband didn't share her faith. Surely that added to her stress at times. Her biggest support appears to have been Timothy's grandmother, Lois, who encouraged her to teach Timothy about Jesus and His love. Maybe Eunice worried about what would happen to Timothy when he grew up. Yet when Timothy became a young man, Eunice released her beloved son to share in the apostle Paul's ministry. (See 2 Timothy 1:5–6 and Acts 16:1.)

Encouragement for You

Welcoming Baby into your home brings new waves of redefined love as well as inevitable change and stress. Because you're human, you (like Eunice) cannot foresee the outcomes of that change. We will wonder about our baby's future. We will wonder whether we are making wise decisions in raising him or her. Our lives will not be stress-free. We cannot guarantee what the father of our baby will do and believe (just like Eunice could not make her husband trust in Jesus).

Yet in 2 Timothy 1:7, Paul gave Timothy great encouragement and as a new mom, this truth is for you, too: "God has not given us a spirit of fear and timidity, but of power, love, and self-discipline" (NLT). Mom, when you're feeling the stress, remember those words.

It's a Juggling Act

Helpful Ideas from Moms

What do you need? What might help reduce your stress levels? Recently some moms shared their thoughts regarding these questions. Which of their ideas fits your situation and might help diminish the pressure you feel? These new moms said:

I need. . .

1. prayer.
2. help with cleaning/cooking.
3. affirmation and encouragement.
4. a way to keep up with my former pursuits, such as a hobby or creative interest related to my previous career.
5. support and validation from my husband that I'm doing a good job with the baby. (Also, regular massages and chocolate!)
6. a friend that I can vent to—one who listens without judging me.
7. to know that it's okay if I don't have the long quiet times and Bible study times that I used to have.
8. ways and methods to help me keep praying throughout my day.
9. a relaxed chunk of time to feed my baby; permission to just sit, rock, rest, and bond with him.

10. assurance that it's all right if my house doesn't have the same neat-and-clean level for at least eighteen more years.
11. a sense of humor.
12. sleep.
13. some mad money to spend on myself.
14. a few hours of alone time occasionally—preferably out in nature, taking a walk or visiting the local park.
15. less structure.
16. more structure.
17. a nanny!

New Moms Need Help Now

If you can manage to get a nanny, more power to you! Actually I recently learned that for years in Europe, families have been hiring doulas to help new moms through the stressful few months after birth. (In some cases insurance paid for it, because the culture recognized the need.) What a lovely, realistic, supportive, and biblical idea. "Do not withhold good from those who deserve it when it's in your power to help them. If you can help your neighbor now, don't say, 'Come back tomorrow, and then I'll help you' " (Proverbs 3:27–28 NLT).

If ever there is a time when someone legitimately needs help, it is after a woman gives birth. Yet, through the decades, we seem to have developed an idea that women can do it all and therefore don't warrant the assistance of others. Inherent in this philosophy is the misbelief that says if you feel stress, there's something wrong with you. Not so. New mom, you are the one who can best determine what you need. If there's an idea in this book that sounds worthwhile to you, go for it. If a particular concept doesn't strike a chord within you, that's fine, too. Simply revel in the fact that you are not alone. Others have experienced what you are feeling as a new mom.

Safe in God's Arms

Messy Love

When you care for your baby you accept the hard stuff, sacrifice familiar comforts, and stay committed when there's no initial evidence of reciprocity. This is love. Messy love. *God-love.*

God showed His massive love for you (and me and your baby and your family) when He sent His Son, Jesus Christ. And Jesus did the hard thing. He left perfection and glory (all that was familiar and comfortable to Him) to live in the midst of injustice, wrong, sin, and abuse. Talk about messy. Messy and stressful.

Then He gave His life that you and I might live and be reconnected to our perfect Creator God. Yet throughout His three-year ministry leading up to His willing death, the compassionate, caring, demonstrative, involved, gentle, strong, revolutionary Jesus spoke truthfully and forcefully to those who mistreated Him.

And His heart broke as they turned Him away. He said, "Jerusalem! Jerusalem! Murderer of prophets! Killer of the ones who brought you God's news! How often I've ached to embrace your children, the way a hen gathers her chicks under her wings, and you wouldn't let me" (Matthew 23:37 MSG).

It's heartrending. *And* it demonstrates the tender love of God for you. For your baby. For your family. In the midst of your changing circumstances and subsequent stress, God wants to gather you under His protective wings. Accept His love.

Close your eyes for a moment. Imagine God holding you. You're safe in His arms.

Our Master Jesus has his arms wide open for you.

1 CORINTHIANS 16:23 MSG

Chapter 9

The Joy of Imperfect Momhood

What's Up, Mom?

Trying Hard to Do It All Just Right

"Is she a good baby?" an older woman asked me—the new youth pastor's wife—on the first Sunday that I took Lynnette to church after she was born. (I'd followed my doctor's rules and waited until my baby girl hit the six-weeks-old mark before I exposed her to all the germs that he said abounded in a church nursery.)

Okay, back to my story. *Is she good? Well, what is that supposed to mean?* I thought. *She's just a baby, after all. What does she know about being good or bad?*

My mind raced with possible responses, and then I got it. *Ohhhh. It's a trick question.* If I said yes, she'd be happy and pleased and I'd sound like a competent and loving mom. Of course, I'd be fibbing, if by "good" she meant that she sleeps all night, doesn't cry during the day especially during our dinnertime, never has a stomachache, doesn't spit up all over her new dress and her dad's good suit when we're late for an appointment, and only poops when it's a convenient time to change her diaper.

But if I replied with no, she rarely lets me sleep and is fussy most of the time and demanding (as my mother said about both my babies), then I'd sound like an ungrateful and complaining new mom. I'd be telling the truth, but. . . *Yes, it's definitely a trick question.*

I sensed that I should maintain a cheerful attitude and a smiling mommy-face, so I think I mumbled, "She's precious and motherhood is a joy!" as I stumbled bleary-eyed to the car. Don't get me wrong, my daughter was then (and still is) precious to me. I was as delighted to be a mommy in those days as I am now. But let's face it, I was one tired, overwhelmed, often alone and unsure of herself, new mommy. Much of the time I felt bullied by the tyrant in my head who droned constantly, *You've gotta try harder to do this all just right, Joan!*

Imagine this or a similar scenario happening at your fitness club or in conversation with your single know-it-all college friends or at a family reunion with your aunt Hildegard and uncle Mortimer—or whatever their names are!

Over-Expectation

Patricia also heard the internal-bully taunts when she came home with her firstborn.

In preparation for my new-mom career, I read all the latest baby-care manuals. I noticed that experts wrote about the attachment theory and how when a baby has his needs met on a regular basis, then baby learns to trust, feels happier and more secure, and grows up to be emotionally healthy.

It made sense to me, so I plunged in with both feet. I jumped every time my little guy cried. Well, actually every time he whimpered or even breathed deeply. What's wrong, honey? What can I get you? How can I make you feel better? What will stop your crying? *I believed I had to do it all just right in order to make sure he turned out just right. But thinking back, I guess I was a bit extreme. (If you asked my family, they might not agree with the "a bit" part!) Oh well. A little balance might have helped us all. I didn't need to nurse him each time he stirred. I think I wore him out with my hovering. I was just so afraid I'd do it wrong.*

Although Sharon identifies with the I-gotta-do-it-right mentality, it just showed up in a little different package for her. "I thought I must show my baby who was the boss right from the get-go. I tried to schedule her feedings and when she wouldn't rest when I needed her to, I let her cry herself to sleep. It broke my heart, but this is what I was instructed to do and I didn't want to make a mistake or go against the rules."

And then there's the mom who wrote a blog about parenting perfectionism. This blogger mom read that pacifiers are bad for her baby's teeth, so she pitched them all and thus had to double her baby's nursing schedule to keep her mommy-sanity. Then a month later she read how experts concluded that pacifiers are fine except for the red ones. She concluded, "We moms have to do it *right*, yet what's *right* is always changing."

Let's face it: We're living in an age of over-information, over-choice, over-tech, and over-expectation. No wonder our internal tyrant is working overtime.

Shoulda-Coulda-Woulda

Maybe you never experienced the Shoulda-Coulda-Woulda Bully, and therefore can't relate to Patricia, Sharon, the blogger, or me. If so, I say, "Way to go, Mommy! Let's do lunch and talk."

Yet if you do understand, even just a smidge, you may have not only tried to do it all "just right," but all on your own, too. Like many moms, maybe you've believed this enticing message of the inner tyrant: *Don't be selfish. You shouldn't bother others with your stuff. You must be strong at all times.*

Joanne admits she gave in to this message at first. When I asked what was most helpful to her as a new mom, she said:

Well, I can tell you what did not *help! Believing I could do it all on my own. I truly expected to be a perfect mom, so I thought I could immediately pick up my career right where I left off. When I had trouble with that, I beat myself up. When I didn't think, feel, or act like I thought I should, I got quite mean to myself. Not pretty.*

Interestingly, what did help me was asking for and accepting help. That was quite the turnaround for an independent, keep-it-all-together, appearance-oriented person like me. What surprised me the most? After humbling myself, crying to my friend, and receiving help, our friendship deepened and I actually relaxed and enjoyed motherhood more.

I learned a major life lesson. I'm not bad for needing help. It's not wrong to ask for what I want. In fact, it's wise. It turned out to be the best thing I could have done for my baby, my man, my career, my family, and myself.

Asking Is Okay with God

Jesus Christ said something similar after He gave His followers the familiar model of the Lord's Prayer. In Luke 11:9 (NIV), He added,

"Ask and it will be given to you; seek and you will find; knock and the door will be opened to you."

If you're like many women I've talked with, you may have the idea that it's not godly or noble to ask others directly for what you need or want. Consequently some moms may retreat or withdraw when feeling neglected or discounted. Others may yell or nag. However, neither way works all that well.

As a new mother, you may be so tired that it's hard to muster the energy to ask for what you want. That's understandable. Perhaps you could share this reality upfront the next time you attempt to voice your needs and request help. Sometimes it's tempting to hold on to the misconception that if someone (often your husband) really cared, he'd figure out what you need and do it for you without you having to ask. Yet when you and I enter into this mentality, it is like we're saying our loved one is a mind reader. And guess what? No other human being has that kind of God-only attribute. Actually, aren't you glad?

At times you may be reticent to ask because you're afraid you won't like the response you get. However, one of the relief-producing truths about relationships is that each person has the right to ask and each person has the right to say yes, no, maybe, or to renegotiate.

God's Invitation to Ask

Perhaps you've had the idea that it's self-centered to bother God with your daily needs. Yet according to Jesus' words, God wants and expects you to come to Him with your requests. One of the most encouraging Bible promises I read as a new mother was Philippians 4:6–7 (NKJV): "Be anxious for nothing, but in everything by prayer and supplication, with thanksgiving, let your requests be made known to God; and the peace of God, which surpasses all understanding, will guard your hearts and minds through Christ Jesus."

God doesn't plan for you to go through this transition into motherhood alone. He knows it's difficult. When you're all worked up from trying too hard to make it all just right, He longs to hold and comfort you like you do your baby when he's upset. So you can take a deep breath and let the tension go. Believe that God is willing and able to help you, and listen to His gentle voice calming you down.

*"The LORD your God is with you,
the Mighty Warrior who saves. He will take great
delight in you; in his love he will no longer rebuke
you, but will rejoice over you with singing."*

ZEPHANIAH **3:17** NIV

Who, Me?

Mr. Should Bully

I sat in the rocking chair, tying bows out of narrow satin ribbon. Every one a different color to match the dresses that Lynnette received as gifts from caring friends. Through sleep-deprived eyes, I maneuvered the slippery ribbon so the finished bow turned out *just so* with a square knot in the front. Then each morning whether or not I took time for a shower or nap, I taped one to her bald head. She looked cute, and I enjoyed this little ritual.

When people asked how we got them to stay on her head, Daddy Richard said with a poker-face, "We thumb-tack them." (Actually, I folded the clear tape into little rolls and put it on the back of each hand-crafted bow. It worked! No one ever saw a clip, barrette—or the tape.) Leave it to Richard to add a little comic relief to our lives. Bless him. I needed it, since my Mr. Should Bully resisted lightheartedness, laughter, or relief.

After all, adhering to those "shoulds, musts, and have-tos" takes time, energy, and concentrated effort. I *should* know better. I *shouldn't* act tired. I *must* get it all done. He *should* agree with me. The baby *should* sleep through the night. I *must not* feel stressed. I *shouldn't* be in pain. I *should* be a better Christian. I *have to* keep up my Bible study.

Making It Personal

Remember that awareness is a key to making relief-producing choices. Throughout the nine chapters of this book we've addressed several specific topics for new moms. Choose one chapter theme and use it as a guide.

Listen to your internal messages. What do you hear? Make a mental or written note of when you're being bullied by a should/must/have-to. Also, note where you're already giving yourself permission to relax and enjoy your good-enough reality.

For example, in the topic related to chapter 3, "Sleepless Nights/Blurry Days," I heard an internal-bully message something like *Joan, you really shouldn't be all that tired. You're a wimp. You need to go to sleep immediately after your baby does.* But trying to live up to this pressure usually meant I lay in bed wide awake and exhausted.

And in my "Learning to Tell Time (All Over Again)" chapter, I gave myself credit for the helpful step I took to manage my foggy thinking. I jotted down what I would otherwise have forgotten and kept the list available. Then I could relax and enjoy the moment without worrying about the next feeding or tomorrow's agenda. *Whew!*

Your Turn

Now it's your turn to choose one chapter's theme and listen to your internal messages about that topic. Follow the directions above and see what you discover.

What did you learn about yourself? I learned that although I could have done a few things a little differently, I did what I could and it was pretty good. *Ahhh. Nice.*

So how will you encourage and reward yourself today? Maybe put a star on your mommy chart. Or buy yourself flowers. Or take an extra nap. Or listen to your favorite musician's latest release. Or call a sitter while you go to the mall for a little while.

Been There—Done That

Blessed Imperfect Reality

Sondra had a dream: to be a mother. A single woman with a high-powered career in the information technology field, she determined to bring her dream to reality, and she did. She adopted two adorable little girls. Although not easy, she succeeded in juggling and maintaining it all. Then life shifted for her and her family. "My life as a mom profoundly changed when I received the news that my precious baby girl had a life-threatening disease," Sondra shared recently. "The things I once thought significant began to pale. Being 'just right' didn't matter anymore. Building and recording family memories became a priority. I hate the disease and what it takes from my beautiful daughter, yet I feel blessed. It's a gift to be reminded to take one day at a time, to not worry so much about tomorrow, and to build precious memories that will last when she is no longer with us."

Sondra's story touched my heart. I've talked with many mommies, and I'm amazed at how resilient and wise they can be—and how they usually sense what they need, even when they think they can't. (There's that inner bully again.)

Here's what Darlene experienced:

I taught special-needs children until the day I delivered Katrina. Then my daily routine changed radically. I had nowhere to go. No one to see. I felt isolated and depressed. A lovely older couple from our

*church knew I loved blueberry muffins, so they brought me one about
three times a week. I wasn't used to accepting help from others, but how
I looked forward to opening that little bag and popping the muffin
into the microwave to warm it up. I threw out my inner message that I
didn't need the extra calories and just let myself enjoy. It became my little
lifeline to the outside world during those difficult months—a special and
practical gift from my loving Father.*

It's a Juggling Act

Comparing No More

Mom, your life has changed and you have a lot to manage. The good news is that you're the one God has placed in charge of your home and baby. Your situation is not exactly like your best friend's circumstances. You have unique needs and so does your baby. No one else has relationships quite like yours.

It's an understandable and wise idea for you to set specific limits on what you will or will not do based on your unique home life. You can still be a loving and giving mom, friend, wife, daughter, and worker when you establish healthy boundaries. This reasonable approach to momhood is okay with God. "Make a careful exploration of who you are and the work you have been given, and then sink yourself into that. . . . Don't compare yourself with others. Each of you must take responsibility for doing the creative best you can with your own life" (Galatians 6:4–5 MSG). Liz understands this.

Liz Turns Off the Noise

I loved being pregnant. I know this isn't the experience of every woman, but I had no nausea, no marriage problems or hormonal imbalances. I talked to my baby throughout each day while I was at work and enjoyed his every roll, twist, and hiccup. I felt special that God had allowed my husband and me to make this amazing little human being living within me. I marveled in my womanhood and felt sad for the male population of the world—that they'd never experience the sheer awe of motherhood.

Then after twenty-eight hours of failed labor and a surprise C-section, our baby son was born. A massive waterfall of emotions overwhelmed me. I felt lost. Questioned every move I made. Didn't understand my child, what he wanted or why he cried. I turned to anyone and everyone I knew for advice—and read book upon book. "No one understands," I said repeatedly. "I'm going nuts." I just could not decipher all the advice.

On Tyler's four-week-old birthday, after an exceptionally long crying fit, I called a dear friend. "Liz, stop!" she said simply. "You know what to do. Listen to your heart. You are Tyler's mother. No one knows what that baby needs better than you."

Oh my. That's right, *I thought. Everything changed. My life as a new mom wasn't suddenly perfect. Yet I started trusting my God-given perceptions and the mother-intuition that has always been there within me.*

I let myself off the I-should-follow-everyone's-rules-just-right hook and began to really believe that God gives women the ability to have a child and all the necessary info (internal instruction manual, if you will) to be a mom as well. I chose not to continue to be confused by all the noisy advice and trusted God to help me be the mother He designed me to be.

You're the Mom; God's Your Helper

The following suggestions are designed to assist you in discovering your unique motherhood needs:

- Ask "What do I really want to do?" When you're in
  quandary about a decision, hopefully your respon
  help you decipher which is *your* desire or need and not
  merely what someone else wants you to do.
- When you get into bed at night, instead of praying, "Lord,
  what did I do wrong today?" and then ruminating about
  what you coulda-shoulda-woulda done, pray, "What did I do
  right, Lord?" Then listen to how God's Spirit prompts you,
  and praise Him for your blessings and His help.
- When you're overly tired, lacking energy, or just plain
  overwhelmed with the mundaneness of mommyhood, ask
  yourself, "Since I'm going to do this activity or task anyway,
  how can I do it easier (or even with a little fun)?"
- Before you get out of bed and/or reach over to pick up your
  baby in the morning, take thirty seconds to talk to God.
  Request His guidance and help for your day. Consider
  asking, "Lord, what do You want to show me today?" Then
  watch for evidence of His love and direction.

God has said, "I will never fail you.
I will never abandon you." So we can say
with confidence, "The LORD is my helper."
HEBREWS 13:5–6 NLT

Safe in God's Arms

You: God's Delight

New mom, God loves you more than you'll ever know. It might be hard for you to imagine, but He loves you even more than you love your baby. Just as you delight in your child and long to keep him safe, warm, and happy, God delights in you (read Psalm 18:19).

God designed you with your personality, gifts, and passions. He's not pushing you to be or do it all perfectly 24–7. At times you may feel a heavy sense of exaggerated responsibility that threatens your joy, yet that doesn't come from God. He just wants to help you be the best version of who He created you to be. He loves seeing you express your unique personhood in your mommy role.

So when you're tired and needing nourishment and assurance, come to God through faith in His Son, Jesus Christ. When your baby's crying. When you question who you are. When you're confused about the decisions you face. When your hormones fluctuate wildly. When you feel disorganized and confused. When you're stressed out. When you're trying too hard to make it all just right. God's invitation stands no matter what the time of day or night. You are not alone.

"Are you tired? Worn out? Burned out on religion?
Come to me. Get away with me and you'll recover
your life. I'll show you how to take a real rest.
Walk with me and work with me—watch how I do it.
Learn the unforced rhythms of grace.
I won't lay anything heavy or ill-fitting on you.
Keep company with me and you'll learn
to live freely and lightly."
MATTHEW 11:28–30 MSG

Scripture
Index

Author Bio

Joan C. Webb, an inspirational speaker and author of twelve books, remembers her "walking zombie" days as a new mom. Joan helps people of all life stages balance self-care with other-care in her role as a life coach. www.joancwebb.com

Notes

Notes

Notes

Notes

Notes

Notes

Notes